Sex Education

Anil Kumar Bhadoria

PEACOCK BOOKS

Published by
PEACOCK BOOKS
7/22, Ansari Road, Darya Ganj,
New Delhi-110002
Phones : +91-11-40775252, 23273880, 23275880, 23280451
Fax : +91-11-23285873
Web : www.atlanticbooks.com
E-mail : orders@atlanticbooks.com

Branch Office
5, Nallathambi Street, Wallajah Road,
Chennai-600002
Phones : +91-44-64611085, 32413319
E-mail : chennai@atlanticbooks.com

Peacock Books is an imprint of
Atlantic Publishers and Distributors (P) Ltd

ISBN 978-81-248-0165-9

Printed in India at Glorious Printers, A-13, D.S.I.D.C.,
Jhilmil Industrial Area, Delhi-110095

Dedicated to

My "Ma" & "Pa"

My Wife "Jyoti"

Bhai "Arun" and "Abhay"
and

Akanksha

Akshay

Alankruti

Ayushi

and

Arjun

Preface

Sex-Practice is everybody's right. To disappoint, majority seek and work for information about sex from immature, ill-informed friends, relatives, colleagues and roadside porn-books and various internet sex-sites. Noting this insufficiency for all students of secondary school and college level, we have attempted to come forward with a concise and comprehensive text covering general as well as essential queries, answers and data. Apart from basic aspects of male and female sexual anatomy, practice of safe sex, family planning, diseases borne out of undesirable sexual practices and various positions for intercourse have been explained. Having observed that the students are invariably unfamiliar with foreplay, orgasm, sex tonics and sexual deviations, a brief description has also been given about each of these aspects.

Discipline is the key to success, which my parents taught me since childhood. I owe everything to my parents, two younger brothers and of course my wife Jyoti who kept motivating me for writing this book.

I am deeply indebted to Dr. Sajive S. Naik, who has been a "Friend, Philosopher and Guide" to me over the years. I owe a lot to Dr. Natwar Sharda, Dr. Nirmal Lakhotia, Girish Garg and Girish Maheshwari who have painstakingly helped me whenever required.

I owe a debt of gratitude to Dr. K.R. Gupta, Chairman, Atlantic Publishers & Distributors (P) Ltd. for publishing this book.

Anil K. Bhadoria

Contents

1

Sex and Education

What is Sex?

Definition of Sex

By Man: Wild and playful fun consisting of hot sweaty, spontaneous and ecstatic exquisite.

By Woman: Serious business.

What is Sex Education?

It is process of acquiring information by young and ignorant people to form scientific attitudes and beliefs about sex, relationships and intimacy through generation of confidence, competencey and knowledge about the Human Body, its genital parts and various sexual processes.

Does Sex Education help?

Yes, Sex Education helps to protect the person from

- Abuse
- Exploitation
- Unintended Pregnancy
- STD (Sexually Transmitted Diseases)
- HIV/AIDS (Human Immunodeficiency Virus)

What, If no Sex Education?

Till late 1990s Sex Education could not get its recognition and every year, millions of youths gather information about Sex

Man Loves to get sex while woman uses sex to get love.

from their innocent uninformed friends or relatives or after some kind of sexual exploitation. "No Sex Education", has prevented any flow of scientific approach towards one of the most talked about subject of life in this universe from toddler to diamond age of 100 years.

How Sex Education works better?

Sex Education helps ignorant young people whether male or female, to

- Differentiate between accurate and inaccurate information.
- Understand social and moral issues involved with sex.
- Discuss sex and sexuality. (Sex is gender while sexuality is gay/straight etc.)
- Understand different cultural attitudes.
- Possess scientific knowledge about pregnancy, abortion, sex determination, and contraception.
- Differentiate between impotency of psychogenic and organic (physical) origin.
- Understand better the concepts of marriage, normal and abnormal sexual behaviour and practices.
- Understand sexual perversion.
- Understand scientifically the 2 different physique and psyche of male and female.

Sex Education at what age should be given?

Females approach puberty early with Budding of Breast tissues (Thelarche) followed by commencement of menstrual cycle (Menarche).

During early teenage, children are curious about physiology and Anatomy of body.

Sensitive and appropriate guidance with scientific touch should be given to children in teenage group, including topics like Pregnancy and marriage to render physical, emotional and intellectual development of young people.

Most Indians use classical missionary position for vaginal intercourse.

College goers and person around 18 should invariably be given knowledge about contraception, pregnancy, abortion and STDs.

Parents as usual are first teachers. A basic presentation should be given by parents for the very spontaneous questions put up by Pre-Adolescent child.

Who should Deliver Sex Education?

Both parents and school. Parents are also to be educated in countries like India through these type of correspondence courses so that they can get their children furnished with scientific and appropriate information about sex and related topics.

Boy should be given information by his father and girl child should be given Sex Education by her mother. Home is the first school and children are open with their parents and it is advisable to lesson first at home than at school.

Should Parents Promote Enquiry?

Parents should not say them, to wait. Proper answers should be given at the time of query by the parents. At school level, for sex education, still much is left for proper teacher-student relationship building. School are required to develop instrumental/pictorial/ photographic approach towards scientific exposure of the sex organs, being briefed by male teachers to male students and so on.

Parent/Teachers discussing sex should observe usage of scientific vocabulary to maintain dignity and respect.

What about Sex Books?

Good and scientific books may fetch personal attention by learner to sex and its fact/myths. Road side sold pornographic books facilitate genesis of unscientific information and beliefs socially as well as morally.

No question about sex should be discouraged to avoid or by not giving an answer. When parents feel uncomfortable with

---

Oral sex is safe and natural.

such questions, they should get in contact with their family physician or a qualified doctor who can brief about the basics of Sexual Anatomy and Physiology.

Questions put up by Adolescent boys and girls shall be attended by their class teachers of Human Science/Biology or if possible a Sex Education symposium can be organised at school/college by qualified Medical Teacher or Doctor. At Rural level School Teachers, Trained Birth Attendants (TBA) or Medical Officer can be of much help.

The strategy to undergo for effective structure for Sex Education is as follows:

- The basic individual school is the home, to settle the very initial queries of the kids. A male child is attracted, first of all to his mother (Oedipus-Complex), while a female child is inclined to her father (Electra-Complex).
- The basic individual teacher is father for boy and mother for girl. The parents are the first educators for children and they have a moral duty to furnish basic structure and mechanism in a very conversational language and in no atypical manner.
- There should be a satisfying answer to each valid query about sex, which should be genuinely true, in modest terminology.
- Young individual found playing with his/her sex organ should not be discouraged or scolded. This only increases the curiosity about their own sex and to the opposite sex. Sex should not be considered as a taboo by the parents and it duly needs an open discussion.
- Every legal question should be satisfied by means of appropriate Ethical, Spiritual and Fundamental answer.
- The questions upheld by children should never be discouraged in any way to produce confusion in mind, which may lead to development of an abnormal concept and genesis of personality disorder in youth.

There are countless women, never had an orgasm yet are happily married.

- The Physiology of birth of baby can be explained by making simple examples of Male-Female plant/tree, thereby explaining if possible as the pollination take place. This possibly is the most appropriate and satisfying way to calm the childhood queries.
- The schools must start conducting seminars and symposiums exclusively on sex to their matriculate students by qualified teachers or doctors, at least twice in a full academic session. These types of sessions can be assisted by Audio-Video presentations also. An open and healthy building of relationship between educator and young students may get them, come forward for even asking or revealing for their perversions also.
- A Free and Open session of Questions and Answers must be there between the educator and young students. The Girls should recieve this session from a female educator only. If this is not possible, then a Male Educator in presence of a senior female class teacher can provide trouble shooting sessions.
- The need is to educate commercial sex workers [CSW] also who are the source of active infection for various sexually transmitted diseases.

How Kids be Informed about Sex?

A step-ladder approach in the family is as under :

3 yrs child	• Always use the right names for sexual organs viz. Penis, Breast, Vulva etc. • Being asked "where do babies come from?", don't describe act of intercourse at this level. Just submit, "Babies grow in a special place inside the mother."
4 yrs old	• By this age, kids are very much attached to their parent. They want to be in bed with parents and may want to see them without clothes even. This can be ascribed

		to physiological development and for avoidance a limit can be set.
5-7 yrs old child	•	Aware of faminity or masculinity.
	•	Shy about asking sexual things.
	•	Sexual fantasy about family members.
	•	Might query about Rape, AIDS or child abuse.
8-12 yrs old child	•	This is the stage of maturing physically.
	•	Pre-teens are concerned much about their normalcy.
	•	Boys have concern about their penis size and girls worry for their breast size.
	•	By 12 yrs, they are ready to know about sex and reproduction.
	•	To be told about sexual and social relations.
Teens 13-19	•	Must learn to say NO and to think twice before saying YES to any tempting offer. (Rule of 2 – think twice)
	•	Need to understand about "Safer Sex".
	•	Must get a good scientifically written book on sex and sexuality.
	•	Must be aware of sexual exploitation and sex diseases.
	•	Reassure the kids that it is normal to masturbate, but with privacy.

Useful Hints for Parents

- Establish open conversational environment with children so that they can share their queries about sex.
- Set Good examples so that kids can see, understand the place of values and morality in life.
- Use correct names of sex organs and sexual behaviors.
- Reassure your kids that they are normal.
- Respect privacy of teen-agers.
- Don't use scare tactics.
- Don't hesitate to admit when you don't know the answer of queries.
- Give just, accurate, short, simple and an honest answer.

2

Human Sex Organs

Female Genital Organ

External (VULVA)

- Mons Pubis
- Labia Majora
- Labia Minora
- Clitoris
- Vagina and its opening.

Internal

- Pair of Ovaries
- Pair of Uterine tubes
- Uterus
- Vagina

Breasts are not included as sex organs as they are secondary sex characters. Breast Tissue consist of 15-20 clusters of Mammary glands enclosed by fatty tissue. These clusters of Breast have secretory cells open at the Nipple which is prominent tip of Breast into which milk ducts open.

External Sex Organs (Fig. 2.1)

Mons Pubis (MONS VENERIS)

Soft and rounded plateau in midline of body at Pubic Symphysis joint being covered with hairs after puberty.

Labia Majora

2 perpendicular folds of skin below Mons Pubis between 2 thighs look like lips are Labia majora. Outer surface of Labia Majora has darker skin and grow hairs after Puberty, while

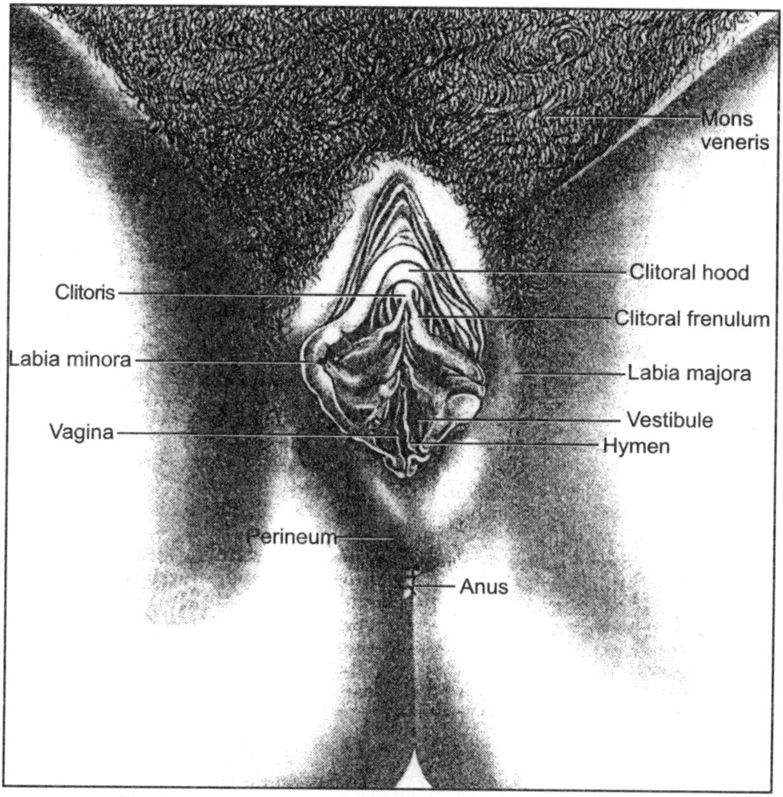

Fig. 2.1: Figure showing Female External Genital Organs

inner surfaces are smooth and hairless. Labia majora consists of set of smooth muscle fibres, nerves, blood vessels and lymph to get it sensitive and sensous to touch, pain, temperature and pressure.

Labia Minora

2 Pinkish, hairless folds of skin between the skin folds of Labia Majora are Labia Minora. Labia Minora enclose vestibule which harbours vaginal, urethral and some ductal openings of Bartholin glands.

Clitoris

Also known as pseudo-penis or penis analogue of females.

This highly vascular structure is enlarged during sexual excitement. It is richly supplied with nerves and vessels to become highly sensitive for sexual stimulation and gratification.

Vaginal Opening

It is externally placed opening visible only when Labia Minora are parted. It is bigger in size and non-gaping.

(B) Internal Sex Organs (Fig. 2.2)

Ovary

Ovaries are 2 in number, meant for production of OVUM. This capsulated organ ovary releases OVUM, being caught by the

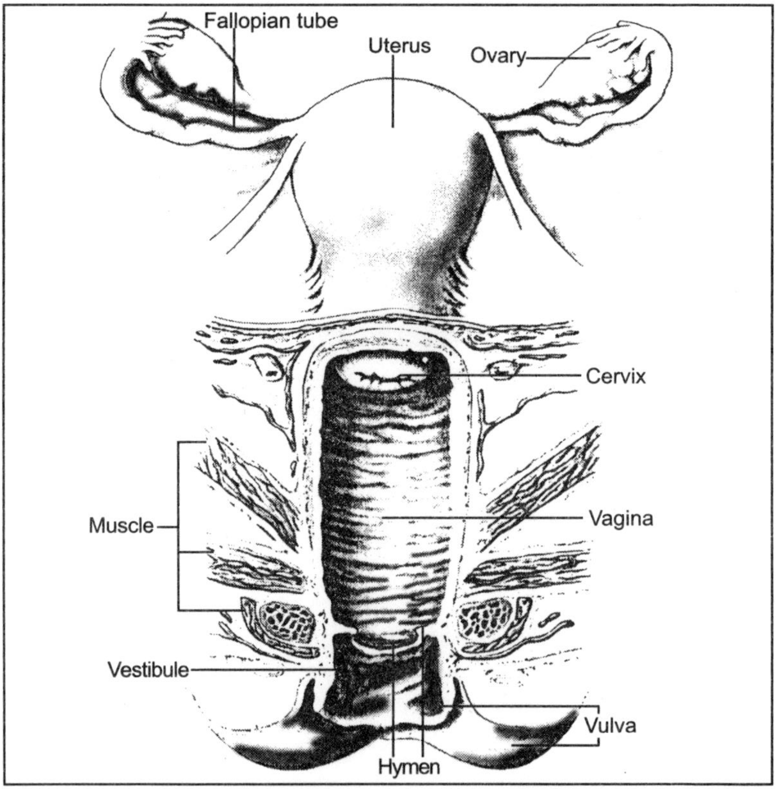

Fig. 2.2: Figure showing Female Internal Genital Organs

Males with excessive non-satiable sex desires are called SATYRIASTICS.

fingered ends of the uterine tubes. Ovary has numerous follicles which release only one OVUM every month.

Tubes of Uterus

Fallopian tubes are about 10 cm. long extending between ovaries and the uterus.

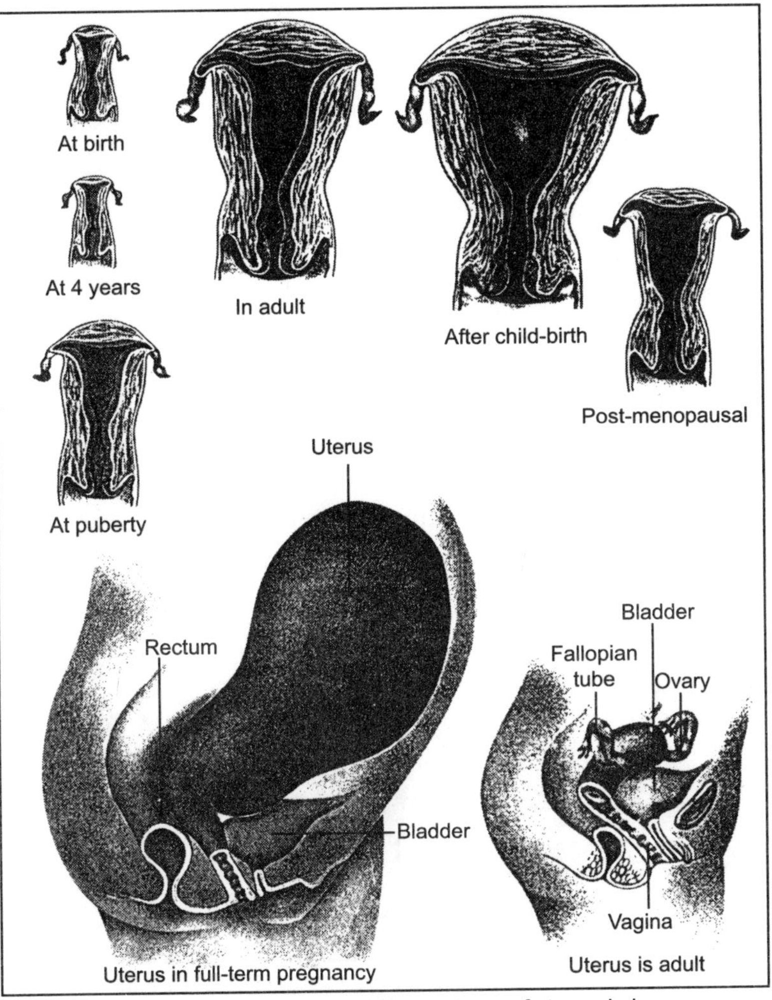

Fig. 2.3: Figure showing different stages of uterus during development and pregnancy.

Fallopian tubes are passages for transfer of OVUM from ovary to uterine cavity

It also traverses the Motile and healthy sperms through to Ampulla part of it to get fusion of OVUM and SPERM which is called as fertilisation.

***Uterus* (Fig. 2.3)**

Uterus is the cavitated muscular organ to harbour and nourish the fertllized OVUM and Embryo, till the birth. The inner cellular coat of uterus is called as Endometrium which sheds its epithelium under the infuence of hormones to release blood through vaginal passage called as menstruation cycle. Average duration of menstrual cycle is 28 days but it may range between 24 to 38 days.

***Vagina* (Fig. 2.2)**

It is main female organ of copulation receiving ejaculate of male called Semen. Vaginal passage is meant to give way to mestrual bleeding every month and to child during birth.

Vagina is a collapsible muscular tube with its upper end communicated with cervix and its canal while the lower end opens between the Labia Minora. Outer 1½ inch of vagina is

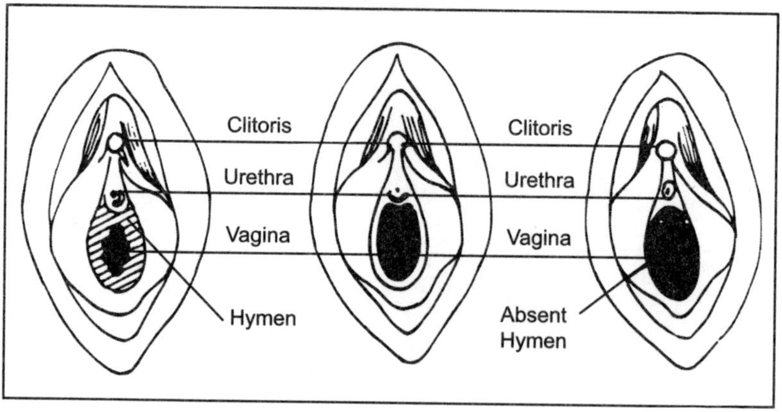

Fig. 2.4: Front Schematic view of Female External Genitalia

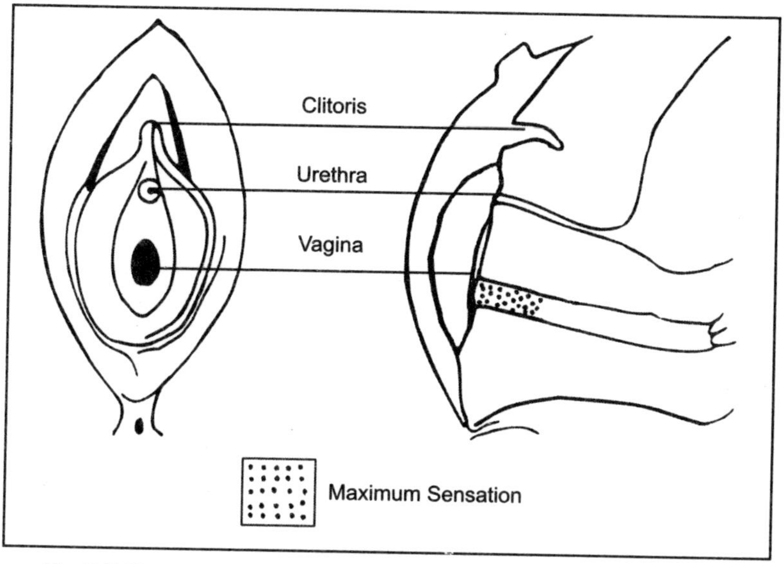

Fig. 2.5: Front and Schematic Coronal view of Female External Genitalia

sensitive to touch, temperature, pain and pressure as it is richly supplied with nerves. Inner part of tube of vagina is all devoid of nerves and therefore is insensitive. It can easily be understood here that to reach orgasm, stimulation of outer 1½ inch of vagina is sufficient. The anterior or front wall of this muscular passage of vagina has specific G-spot in its outer 1 inch which helps attaining the orgasm if stimulated properly during masturbation or in vaginal intercourse.

Male Genital Organ

External	*Internal*
• Penis	• Testes
• Scrotum	• Prostate
	• Seminal Vesicle
	• Cowper's glands

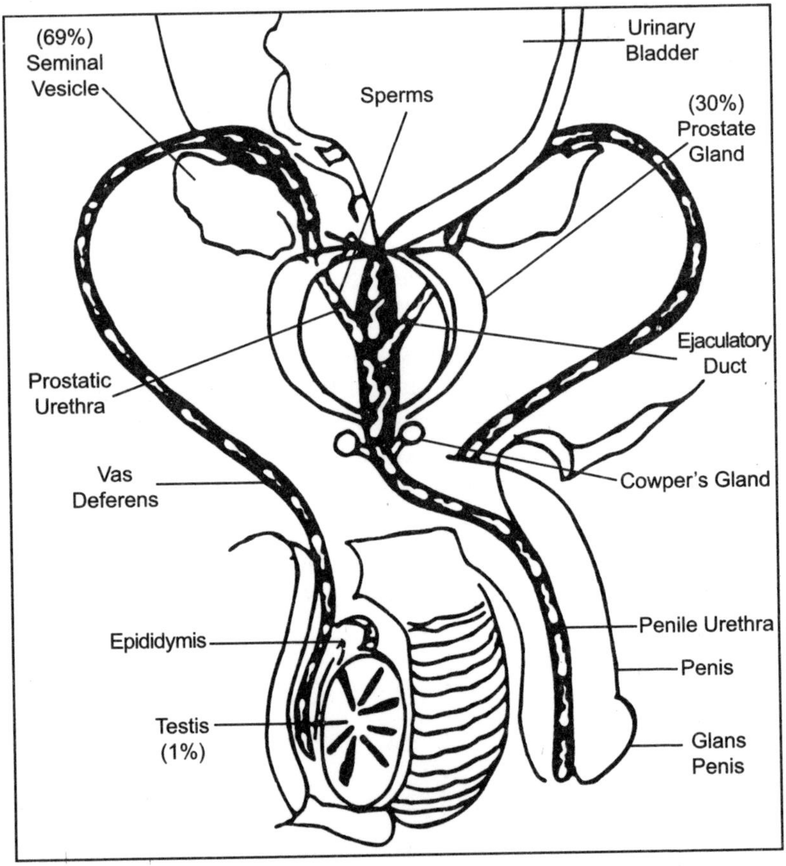

Fig. 2.6: Showing Male Internal Genitalia with movement passage of sperms. (%) show part of secretion in Semen Ejaculate.

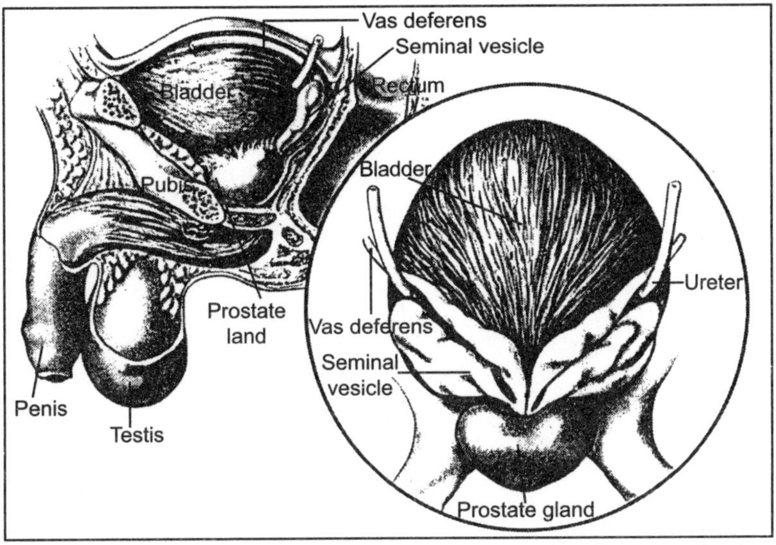

Fig. 2.7: Showing Male Genitalia with organs and position of prostate gland

External Sex Organs

Penis (Fig. 2.12)

It has a free hanging part called body and an attached part to anterior pelvic wall called Root. The tip part of Penis is known as Glans Penis where an opening is present to urinate and ejaculate the semen called External Urethral Meatus.

Glans is shiny, pink and sponge like globular organ sensitive to touch. It is devoid of hairs or any sweat gland, being covered by a fold of skin called foreskin or prepuce.

Length of Penis

Soft Penis (flaccid) has a length about 8 cm. to 12 cm. The Penis has no bone or cartilage in it to cause erection. After erection, the length of Penis varies between 12 cm. to 18 cm.

State of Penis (Avg. values)	*Flaccid*	*Erect*
Length	8-12 cm.	12-18 cm.
Diameter	2-3 cm.	3-5 cm.

The act of sex is enjoyment second only to laughing.

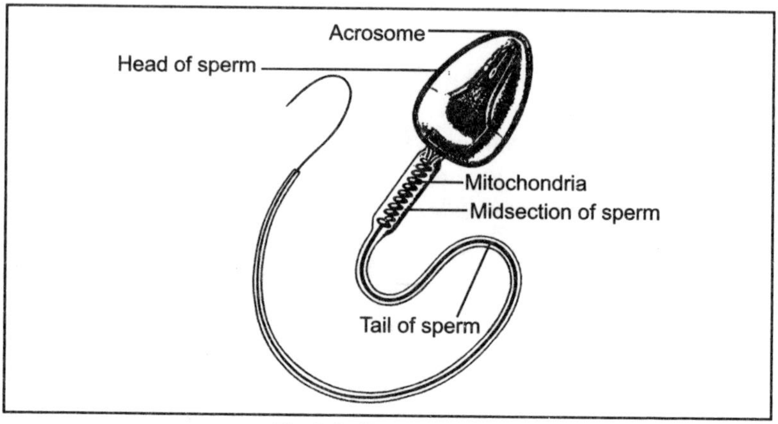

Fig. 2.8: Showing sperm

Straightness of Penis varies just as the height vary from person to person. Normal Penises are all straight and slightly curved. Penises curved to right or to left also are normal. It is not the length but breadth which helps much to reach the orgasm.

Erection (Fig. 2.10)

Phenomenon of erection is regulated by dilatation of blood vessels in Penis, into which blood flows.

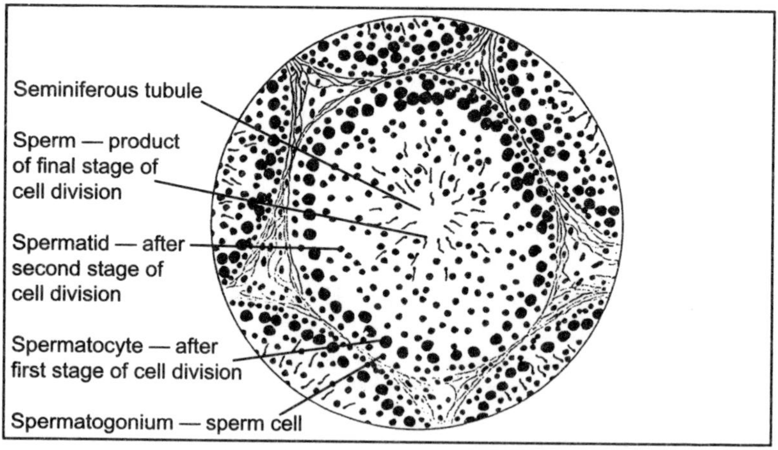

Fig. 2.9: Showing spermatogenesis

Sperm can live up to five days inside a woman's reproductive system.

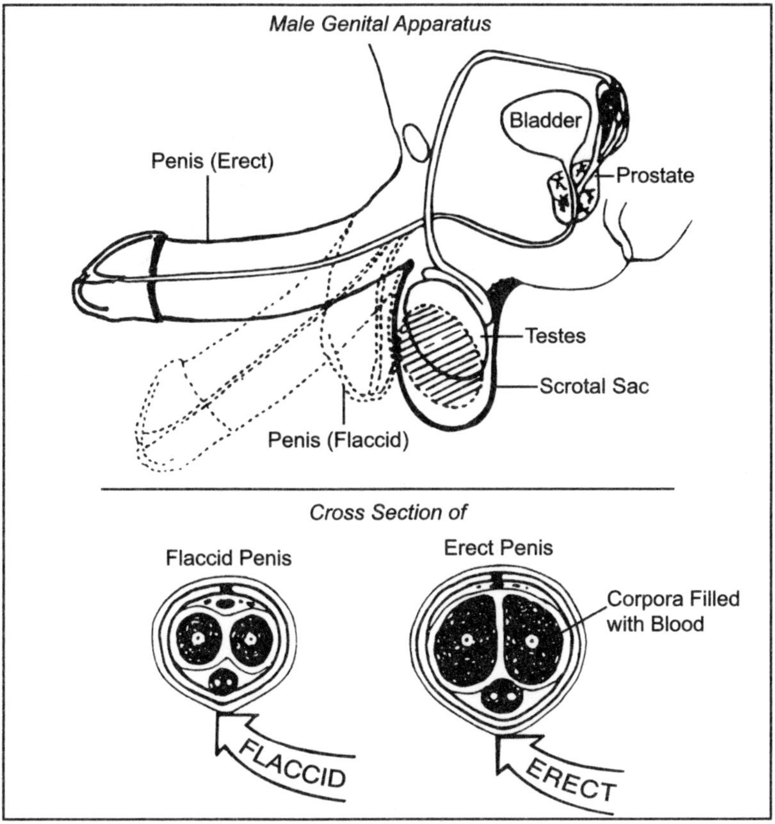

Fig. 2.10: Showing mechanism of Erection of Penis.

Development of erection takes place when space in erectile tissue is flooded with blood at a rate of 20-60 ml. per minute. Orientation and initiation of erection is induced at 2 levels in body namely:

1. Psychogenic Erection

Which is stimulated by seeing, feeding, reading, and thinking.

2. Reflex Erection

Spinal cord mediated erection act by touching or stimulating the genitals which reflexly stimulate sacral part of spinal cord, thereby leading to erection.

Sex is not only physical event but emotional and psychological too.

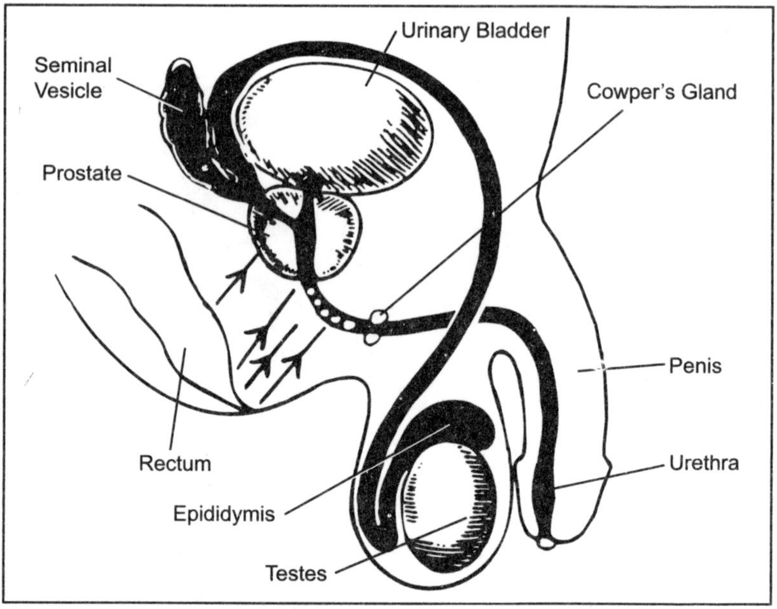

Fig. 2.11: Diagram showing organelles producing secretions for semen and lubrication.

	Psychogenic Erection	*Reflex (Physical) Erection*
• Result of	Stimulation from Brain	Direct —Physical Contact
• By Means of	Fantasy Visual Stimulation	Touch —Penis, Ears, Neck, Breast
• Act is	Voluntary	Involuntary
• Stimulating Sexual Thoughts	Always Present	May be Absent

Act of Sex is an art and the length of Penis does not regulate the satisfaction in sex. There are multiple factors involved in attainment of orgasm in males and females that determine reaching the heavenly point of orgasm.

Female seeks love while male seeks body in sexual relation.

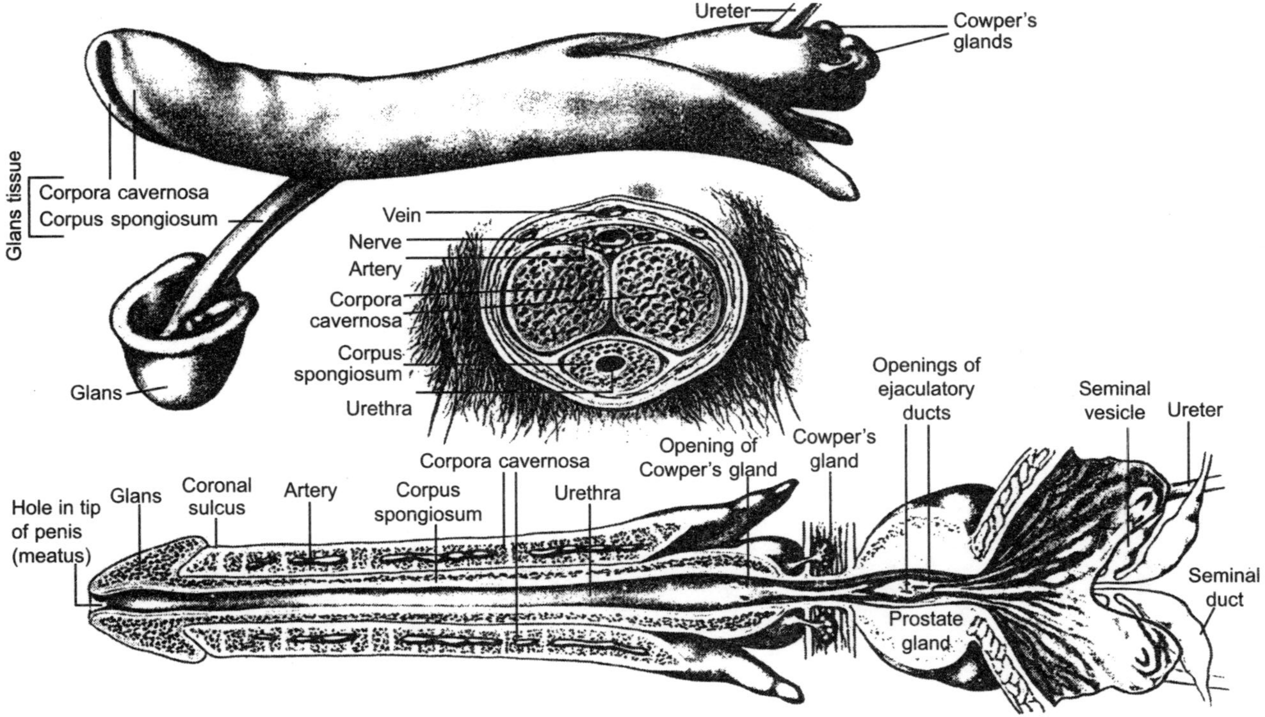

Fig. 2.12: Showing Schematic Separation of different parts of Penis. Cut Sections in Transverse and in coronal plane also are displayed, along with glands.

These factors are:

1. Foreplay
2. Environment
3. Relationships
4. Time of act
5. Anxiety
6. Fear
7. Pre-occupation
8. Diseases e.g. Diabetes, Infection
9. Stress
10. Inhibitions
11. Hormonal Imbalance
12. Drugs

***Scrotum* (Fig. 2.13)**

It is a loose bag of tortuous skin, having 2 chamber into which 2 right and left testes (Testicles) are suspended, with the help of spermatic cord.

Extra abdominal placement of testes in scrotal sac facilitate suitable maintenance of temperature about 1-2° lower than normal body temperature of 37°C. Sperms produced in testicles are stored at superior pole of testes at 34-35° or even less temperature. High temperature in and around testes have been reported to cause sterility.

Internal Male Organs

Testes

Present in scrotal sac 2 in number. Left testis being heavier is placed at a low level than right testis.

Functions of Testis

1. Production of sperms since pubery to death (Spermatogenesis) Fig. 2.9. The normal rate of production of sperms in 2 testes is about 40-50 thousands per minute. (Fig. 2.8)
2. Production of male sex hormones (Androgens) namely Testosterone.

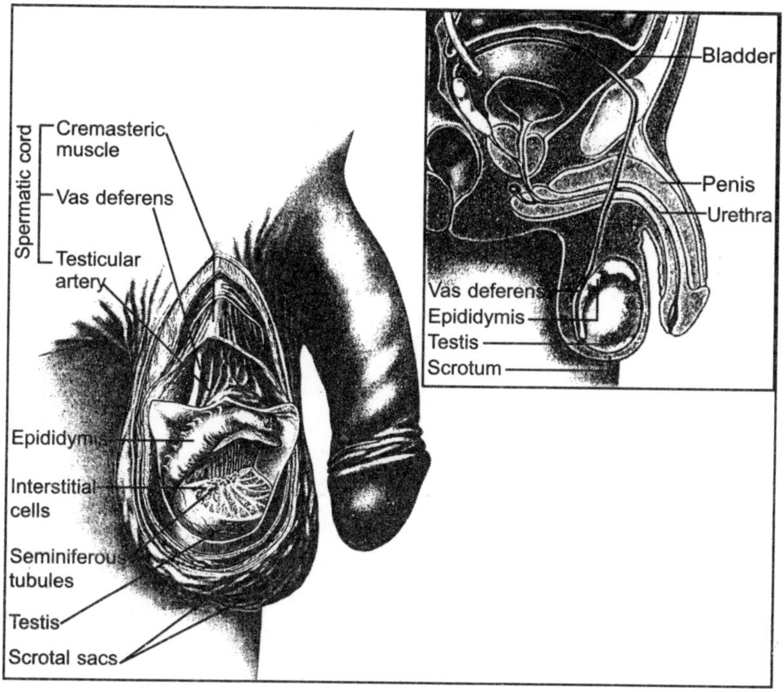

Fig. 2.13: Showing Structure of Testes and Duct System of Male Genitals

Semen

It is the alkaline, protein rich ejaculate from Penis consisting of secretions from the following:

Name of gland	*Secretion Content*	*Quantitative fluid*	*Function*
Testes	Sperms	5%	Fertilization
Prostate	Nutritive fluid	30%	Nutrition and mobility of sperm
Seminal Vesicle	Fructose	60%	Fructose rich facilitate nutrition and mobility
Cowper's gland and Bulbourethral gland	Lubricating fluid	5%	Lubrication

For man, sex cannot be just insertion and ejaculation.

3

Developmental Phases in Human Body

Adolescence

This period lasts between onset of puberty to sexual maturation of boy and girl child.

Puberty/Adolescences begins early in girls by 10 years (8-13 Yrs.) and boy by 12 yrs. (10-15 Yrs.)

Pubertal development is initiated by an endocrine gland present in brain called Pituitary gland and it is controlled by Hypothalamus.

Sexual development in adolescent girls occur as:

(a) Firstly breast development. (Thelarche)

(b) Development of Pubic hair.

(c) Menarche, normally 2 yrs. after development of Pubic hairs, is commencement of Menstrual Cycle.

Sexual development in males:

(a) Enlargement of testes and scrotal sac.

(b) Enlargement of hairs.

Menstruation (Fig. 3.2)

Reproductive age of a female is in between 15-45 yrs. Commencement of menstrual cycle which is monthly discharge of blood from vagina is menarche. Cessation of menses is known as Menopause. The age of menarche is about 12-15 yrs. while of menopause is 47-52 yrs.

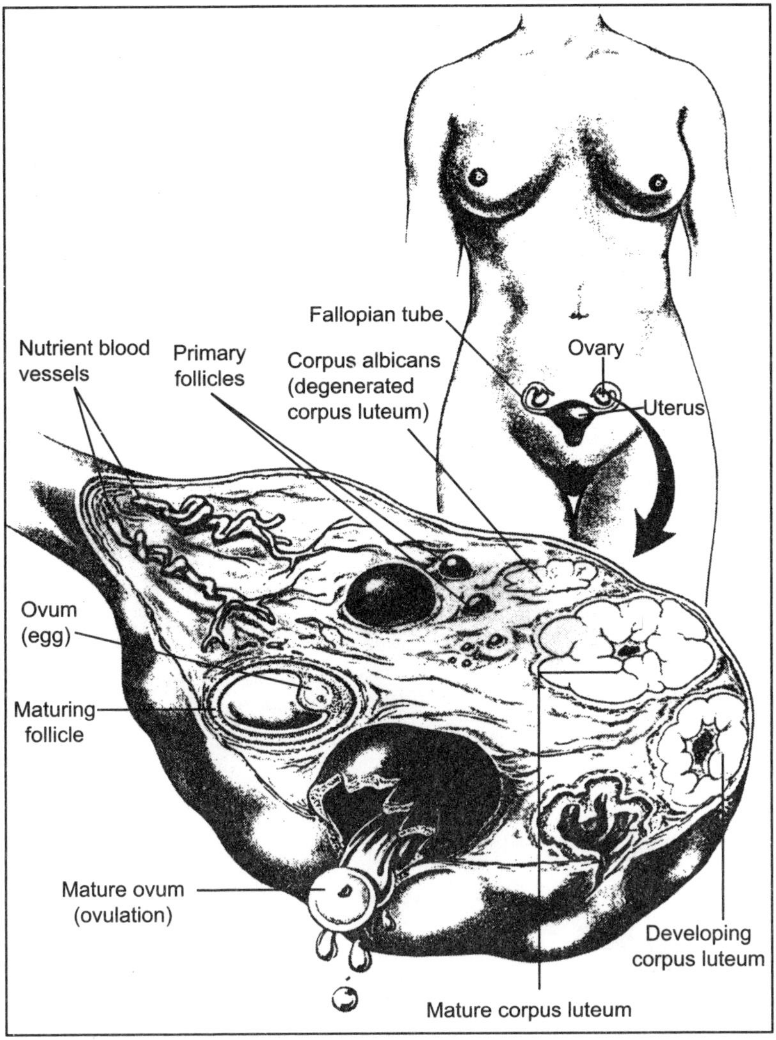

Fig. 3.1: Showing different stages of maturation of Human Ovum in Ovary

The average span of menstrual cycle is 28 days which may extend between 20-35 days period. Menstrual cycle is regulated by 2 female sex hormones called *Estrogen* and *Progesterone* which are produced by 2 ovaries (Fig. 3.1). Ovaries function under control of 2 hormones released from Master gland of body in brain namely FSH and LH. Under hormonal influence the endometrial cell layer of uterine cavity disintegrates and sheds itself with blood. This blood is discharged through canals of cervix and vagina. This monthly discharge normally is about 50 ml./day lasting for 3-5 days. Onset of menstruation is final indication of womanhood.

Pregnancy

Pregnancy is one of the most serious sexually transmitted condition. Pregnancy is a result of union of sperm with OVUM. OVUM are female agency released from ovaries in fallopian

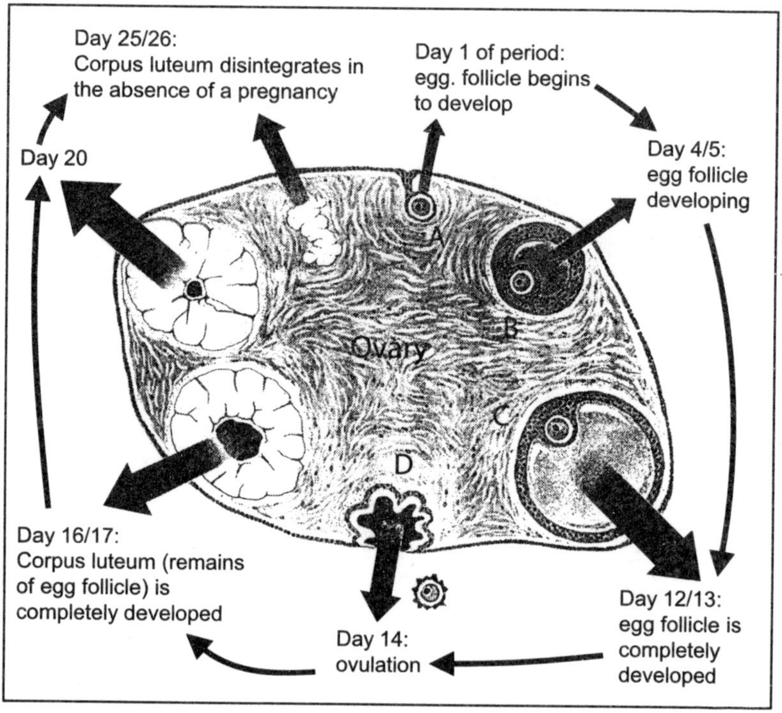

Fig. 3.2: Day Cycle presentation of Menstruation and Ovulation.

tubes, having configuration of 23x chromosomes and a life span of 24-36 hrs. (Fig. 3.1)

Sperms are male counterparts for pregnancy, produced in Testes and are deposited at the mouth of uterus through ejaculation, each having a configuration of 23x chromosomes and a life span of up to 5 days, in female reproductive tract.

Fertilization (Fig. 3.3)

It is a phenomenon of penetration of sperm into the OVUM, after intercourse. Fertilization occurs in fallopian tube within 24 hrs. of release of OVUM from ovary. Normally it is just one

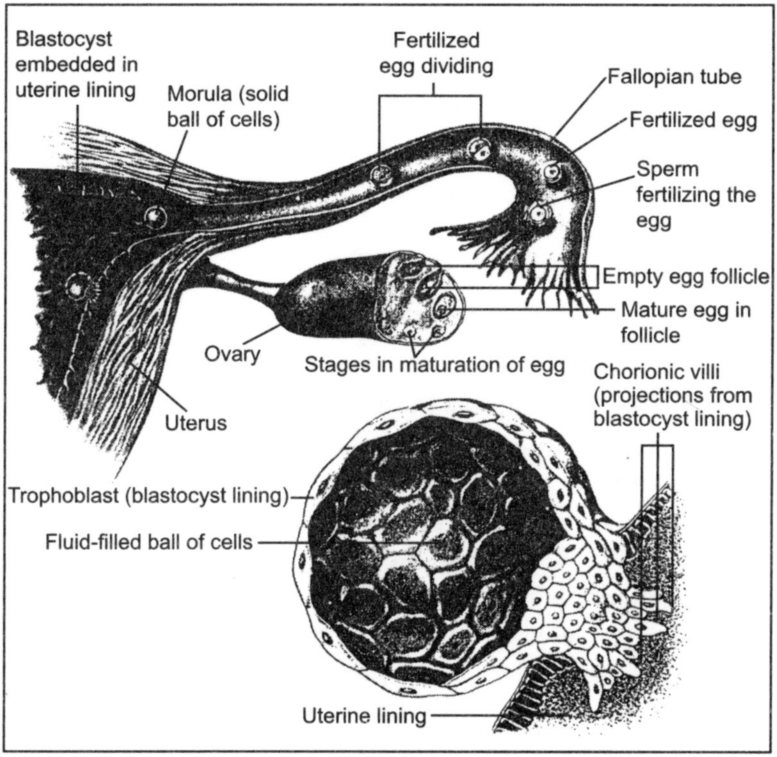

Fig. 3.3: Showing movement path of unfertilized and fertilized ovum through to fallopian tube.

active and motile sperm which penetrate the membrane to enter the OVUM.

A human cell has 46 chromosomes. Meeting of sperm with OVUM produce a complete single cell of 46 chromosomes called Zygote. This Zygote in fallopian tube divides to split into 2 to 4 to 8 to 16 to 32 to 64 cell stage, till it reaches the cavity of uterus. Once in uterus it is called as Blastocyst. The inner lining of uterine cavity is called as Endometrium which receive the fertilized egg, now called Blastocyst. This Blastocyst is implanted in Endometrium.

After implantation only; one is said pregnant or conceived. After implantation of fertilized egg (Blastocyst) endometrium does not shed under hormonal influence, leading to a missed period, very simply been understood with Pregnancy.

Five basic early signs of Pregnancy are:

(1) Amenorrhoea i.e. Missed Menstrual monthly cycle.

(2) Morning Nausea.

(3) Darkened Areola of Nipple.

(4) Full and Tender Breast.

(5) General fatigue.

Gender Deciding Factors in Pregnancy

Every human cell has 46 chromosomes which divide to multiply with two ways:

(a) Mitosis in which cell division is with no change in number of chromosomes in dividing cells.

(b) Meiosis in which cell division is with carrying of half number of chromosomes in daughter cells.

The division of cells to produce sperms and OVUMs is by this meiosis method, through which OVUM carry 23x chromosomes and sperms carry 23x or 23y chromosomes. Sperm are configured with 22 Autosomes and 1 sex chromosome which decide the sex of the fetus.

Rape is a crime against human, not against hymen.

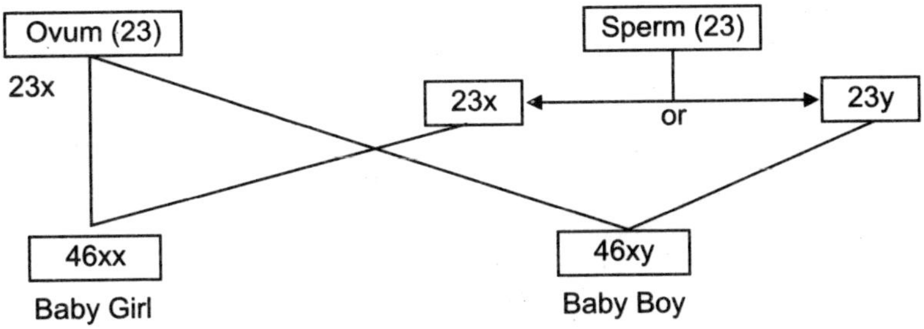

The figure simply explains the sperm containing Y chromosome penetrating OVUM will produce baby boy and likewise baby girl.

4

Sexual Response

It is the brain which regulates desire of performance of sex in male. Brain controls the genitalia through its nerve connections via spinal cord which is present in vertebral column and through blood via hormone release. This way we have 2 channels of control (a) Neurological and (b) Hormonal. Hypothalamus is the part of brain which is main centre of controlling reproduction and related activities. Hormones are chemical substances released from glands present in body, regulating various activities of metabolism, growth and reproduction of human body.

Factors Causing Sex-Stimulation

The stimulation about sex is received from various following factors:

(a) Physical contact (Touch).

(b) Vision.

(c) Smell.

(d) Fantasy/Imagination.

(e) Hearing.

(f) Reading about sex stories.

It is rightly said, the site of sex is not between the legs but between the two ears.

Abstinence i.e. waiting to have sexual intercourse is the best overall choice for teens, preventing both pregnancy and STD and above all, the character of a person.

Hormones and their Role in Sex

The desire of sex is regulated by Androgens (Hormones) which are secreted from testes and ovaries. Hormone is a substance secreted by a gland and is carried elsewhere through circulation to influence the function of specific cells or organs.

The following hormones have a positive or negative effect on puberty, sexual desire and pregnancy.

Hormone	Released from	Effect
1. Follicle stimulating hormone	Pituitary gland	• Stimulate follicle of ovary to mature ova.
2. Leutinizing hormone	Pituitary gland	• Stimulate sperm production in males. • Stimulate ovulation in females.
3. Testosterone	Testes in males, Adrenal gland in both sexes, Ovaries in females	• Male secondary sex characters male sex desire. • Female sex desire.
4. Estrogen	Ovary	• Female secondary sex characters • Regulation of menstrual cycle
5. Progesterone	Ovary	• Breast development • Endometrial development in uterus.

Sexual Responses

Brain has 2 large cerebral Hemispheres which is the head-quarter of all human activities. The cerebrum controls sexual responses through centres in spinal cord. The vertebral column of human being has a canal in which spinal cord is protected and gives out various peripheral nerves, which are like electrical wirings. These nerve fibres message the impulses to and from muscles, joints and skin, from/to brain.

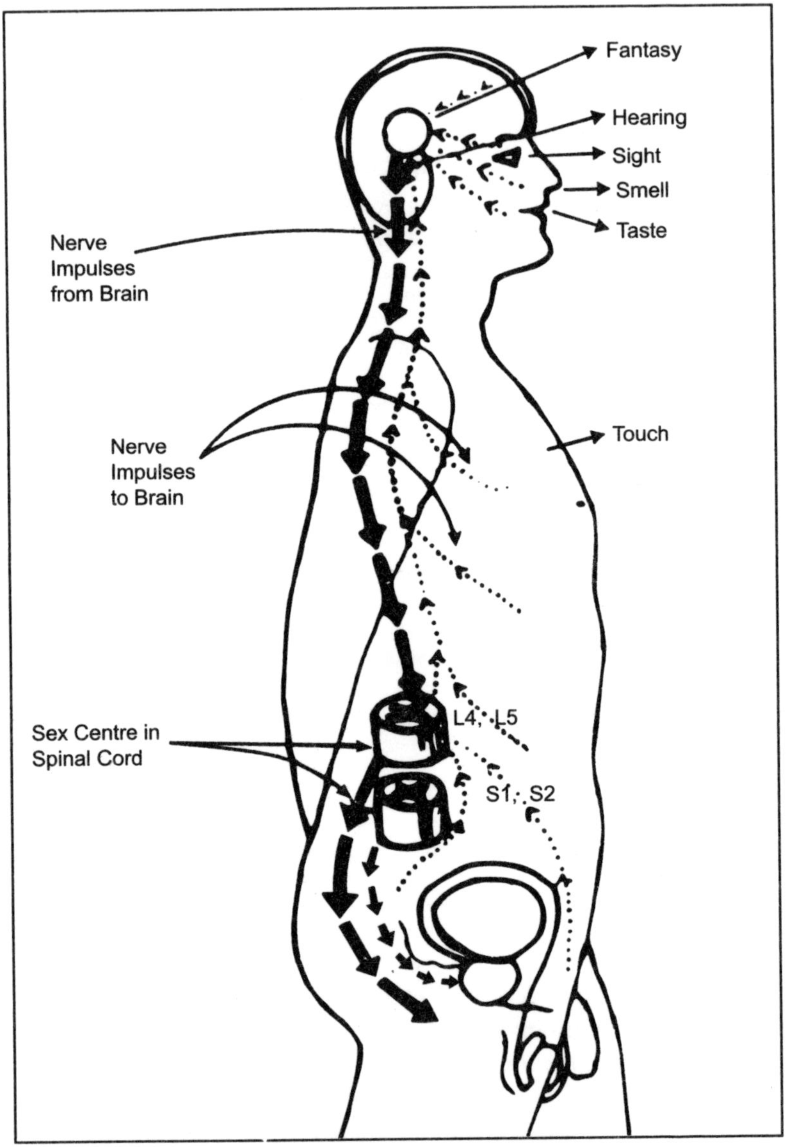

Fig. 4.1: Male Sexual Response
Dotted Arrows show Trigger points
Wide Arrows show Flow of Sex Response.

Men can use masturbation to control their orgasm.

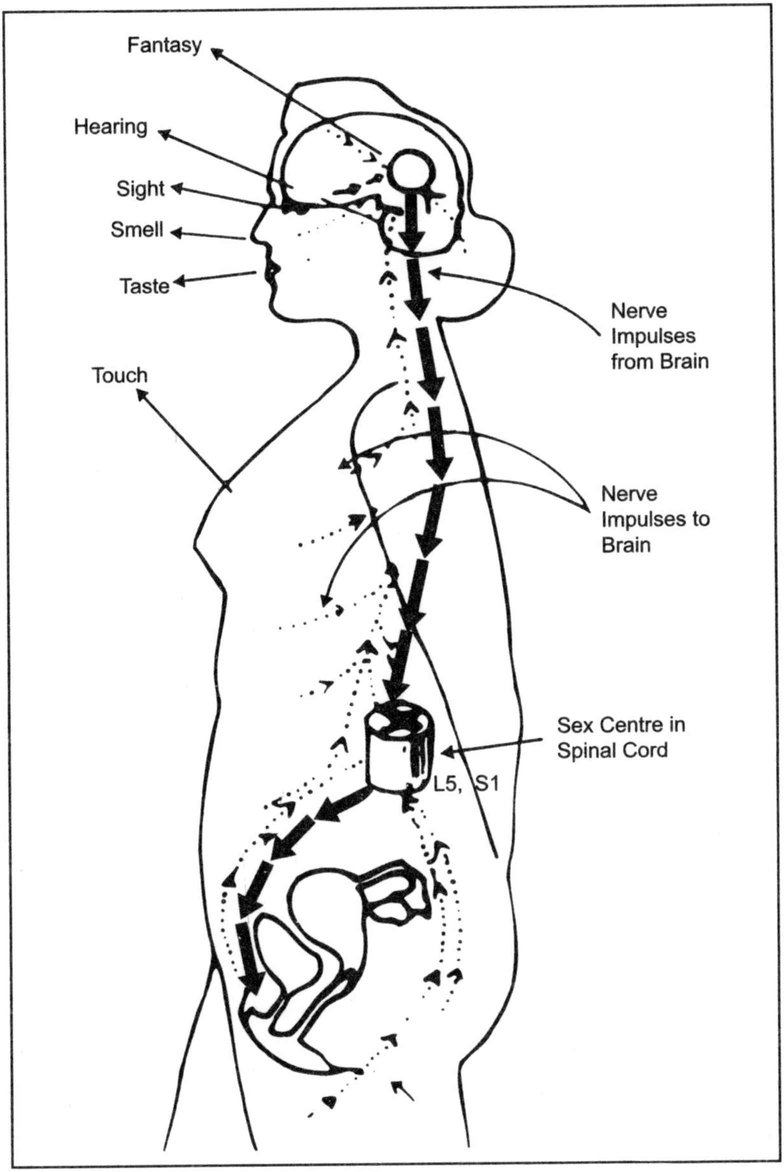

Fig. 4.2: Female Sexual Response.

Women can use masturbation to have their orgasm more easily.

The sex response in males and females consists of different phases namely:

I.	*Phase of Excitement*	Which is characterised by increased Heart Rate, Blood Pressure, Respiratory Rate.
	Duration	Minutes to Hours
II.	*Phase of Plateau*	Which is surge of sexual tension. Intense and Brief;
	Duration	1-10 minutes.
III.	*Phase of Orgasm*	It is release of Endorphins and Ejaculation.
	Duration	Shortest 1-10 seconds.
IV.	*Phase of Resolution*	It is cooling down period.
	Duration	10-20 minutes.

Physiological Changes in Various Sex Phases

Male	*Female*
1. Excitement Phase • By physical and psychological factors. • Penis Engorges. • Skin of Scrotum Contracts and thickens. • Testis is drawn up. • External urethral meatus receives, produce of cowper's gland to lubricate urethra. • Heart rate increased. • Blood pressure increased. • Tone of muscles of Abdomen, chest and thighs is increased.	1. Excitement Phase • By physical and psychological responses. • Sex flushes appear as mild rash in chest, neck and anterior abdominal wall. • Nipple erection, takes place. • Skin around nipple called Areola enlarges by 20%. • Tension/contraction of muscles of Arm, Chest, Abdomen and legs is increased. • Heart rate increased. • Blood pressure increased. • Vaginal passage is lubricated.

If you want to have sex, you should have it always with one but it would be better if you had it with none.

Male	*Female*
2. Plateau Phase • Size of testes is increased by 50% because of increased blood supply to the area. • Penis still enlarges, with flooding of blood into 2 corpora. (See Fig. 2.10) • Glans become reddish purple, may emit few drops of seminal fluid meant for lubrication.	2. Plateau Phase • Due to increased blood supply in and around vaginal passage, vestibule the vaginal opening is reduced by 50% in size. • Contractility of muscles of thigh and buttock is further increased.
3. Orgasm Phase Orgasm is release of Semen through external Urethral meatus after Propulsive rhythmic contraction of muscles. This rhythmic contraction takes place at an interval of 0.8 sec. Single act of intercourse or ejaculation leads to single orgasm.	3. Orgasm Phase Orgasm in females is not like discharge of any kind, through urethral or vaginal opening. Orgasm here is intense ending of arousal and desire like flash of a light in flash of a second. The muscles in this phase respond by involuntary contraction of multiple muscle groups. This is accompanied by release of Endorphin throughout body. Endorphin is a pain relieving physiological substance. Orgasm in females is of 2 types: (a) Clitoral (b) Vaginal or G-spot. Multiple orgasm in a single act of inter course can be achieved in cases of females.
4. Resolution Phase • Ejaculation leads to lost erection of the penis • Sexual desire is lost. • Scrotum and testes return to their normal sizes. • HR, BP, RR reaches normal.	4. Resolution Phase Resolution in females is with: • Relaxation of muscles. • Fading of flush. • Fading of nipple and clitoral erection. • HR, RR and BP reaching normal.

Aphrodisiacs are agents known to enhance sexual desire and performance.

Male	Female
• Resolution phase is followed by refractory period in which erection again is achieved. This period increases with age of person i.e. young age has less refractory period and vice versa.	• Labia size returns to normal.

* HR – Heart rate
* BP – Blood Pressure
* RR – Respiratory Rate

5

Sex Activities

Seven kinds of sexual activities are preferred by males and females:

1. Intercourse
2. Masturbation
3. Oral Sex
4. Rectal Sex (Anal)
5. Nocturnal Sex Dreams
6. Homosexuality
7. Sex Deviations

Sex Desire

It is regulated by hormones released from Anterior Pituitary gland, Testes and Ovaries.

The desire of sex whether increased or decreased can be of psychogenic or organic origin.

Increased sexual desire may be due to alcohol ingestion, addiction of marijuana or other addictive drugs/Herbal Plants, tumors of frontal lobe of cerebrum, after head injury or in temporal lobe epilepsy. Psychogenic states of mania, schizophrenia or a long duration of abstinence may also increase the sexual desire.

Decreased sexual desire may psychologically be due to Depression, Anxiety, stress, schizophrenia, interpersonal

---

Intercourse is more of a quality concern than quantity.

relationship or even dislike of partner. Organic cause to decreased libido may attribute to some medicines, diseases of Liver and Testes in males, or chronic debilitating illness.

Vaginal Intercourse

Definition – It is the act of inserting the penis into the vagina for enjoyment and for causing pregnancy.

Intercourse

Man loves to get sex while woman uses sex to get love. Intercourse is not what man does to woman or woman does to man but a sexual activity, man and woman do, to each other. Intercourse is defined as penetration of penis into the vagina to deposit semen to conceive and to reach orgasm.

Penetration of penis into anal entry is termed as anal intercourse. Intercourse is the most pleasurable experience that people can share. This act of sex is the way of enjoyment second only to laughing.

The Method

The excited and hardened penis is inserted into vagina to stimulate the sensitive areas of the vagina and penis. The stimulation is facilitated by movements of penis or of vagina while keeping the counterpart as stationary, or both can be set on movement to find the most formidable enjoying experiences.

The most sensitive part with vagina are :

1. Lower or outer 1½" of vagina.
2. G-spot in front wall of vagina.

The most sensitive part with penis are :

1. Glans penis.
2. Under surface of shaft of penis.

Intercourse whether vaginal or anal is all about movements, which may be slow or quick or interrupted. Movements of forward and backward nature facilitate the most sensitive parts of vagina and penis to try to reach the most ecstatic feeling of orgasm. The movements of penis and vagina in unison help sharing of the experience. For better sex it is individual's choice to thrust fast or slow or remain idle after deep penetration to reach climax. A proper mixture, and variation in depth of penetration stroking speed and rhythm is all to give a different feel, everytime intercourse is done.

Various positions have been practised since ancient time and have been a matter of discussion. Movement of penis actively or receiving it passively is the crux of attainment of enjoyment in coitus. Rhythmic to and fro movements of penis at slow or fast pace gives heavenly pleasures. The movements could be:

(a) Slow and rocking.

(b) Quick and shallow.

(c) Simple deep penetration, with slow and shallow movements.

(d) Stroking with complete expulsion of penis for multiple entries into vagina.

(e) Quick and deep strokes.

Vaginal intercourse is assisted by foreplay in which stroking, blowing, kissing, licking, sucking of various human organs is done before actual vaginal intercourse is commenced and done.

Frequency of Coitus– Frequency is dependent on physical fitness and is dependent on desire. Age of male/female partner does play an important role in determining the frequency of intercourse. A survey shows weekly frequency of marital coitus as under:

Age	*Frequency of Marital Coitus*
• 17-25 yrs.	5-6 times/week
• 26-34 yrs.	4-5 times/week
• 35-44 yrs.	2.0 times/week
• > 45 yrs. and above	1 time/week to 1 time/two weeks.

As is understood the phases of excitement, plateau and orgasm is followed by refractory period. This refractory period is the time elapsed after reaching an orgasm, before man can achieve and manage another phase of excitement, plateau and intercourse. In early teens this refractory period may not be more than few seconds, thereby leading to high frequency of intercourse. This refractory period lengthens with age, as under:

Age	*Duration of Refractory Period*
• 25-30 yrs	About 15-30 minutes
• 30-40 yrs	About 30-120 minutes
• 40-50 yrs	About 12-24 hours
• >50 yrs	About 01 day to 15 days

Masturbation

Definition – It is a solo act of sexual organ fondling to reach self gratification or auto-eroticism as a supplement or substitute for actual coitus, done both by males and females, more in youngsters.

Literal meaning of Masturbation (Latin) is to defile with hands.

It is not a harmful act as it is thought. It does not cause any physical injury whatsoever in routine way. *It is a habit not a disease.* Virtually all men do this physiological act with some regular or irregular regularity. During actual sexual act what a penis does in a woman's vagina, it experiences in the folded palm during masturbation. It is also very easily understandable that intercourse does no harm to reproductive organs, so does masturbation. Rather intercourse cause pregnancy while masturbation get you to reach only orgasm and no pregnancy. Some religions quote this act as sinful and heinous and solicit confession. Masturbation truly is both physically and mentally satisfying, as well as spiritually fulfilling, having no hazardous effect at body or psyche. Masturbation is a perfectly legitimate form of sexuality. It is sex, just "Sex for one."

Benefits of Masturbation

Masturbation brings:

1. Self satiety of sexual desire.

2. Ejaculation which gives due orgasmic feel rendering prevention of the subject to go for professional sex workers.
3. Prevention from sexually transmitted infections.
4. Prevention from Pregnancy.
5. Society ethics and cultures can be maintained by this act of self-enjoyment.
6. Improvement with premature ejaculation and holding of ejaculation for some time.
7. Sexual frustration to be kept at low level with masturbation.

Adverse Effects of Masturbation

There is no negative side effect associated with masturbation whatsoever physically. Lack of information about pros and cons of Masturbation may lead to Psychological disturbances in youngster's mind.

Myth and Facts About Masturbation

1. Men are given with semen for about 700 ejaculate only in the life?

Ans. Sperm and viscous fluid of semen is produced in Testes, prostate and seminal vesicles. Its production starts at puberty and lasts till old age around even 100 yrs. It is a continuous process. The myth is false about number of ejaculate in a life of man.

2. Is Excessive Masturbation harmful?

Ans. Controlled Masturbation in either sex is not at all harmful to physique of subject. But psychological compulsion for Masturbation may lead to hampered emotional, physical and psychological health.

3. What is normal frequency of Masturbation?

Ans. There is no such fixed number for healthy sex activity with Masturbation. It all depends on the Sex Appetite/ Desire/Eroticism or appeal for sex which varies from

A person can get Condoms, Diaphragm, Jelly, Foams and Suppositories without a prescription from a drug store.

person to person. Masturbation is just like being hungry as you fill the stomach with variety of foodstuff. Likewise the Eroticism of psyche renders to lead this phase of self gratification.

4. Should Masturbation necessarily be done?

Ans. It is not necessary but possibly all men do practice it or have practiced it in their life for some time. Females also practice but it still is somewhat a taboo. Masturbation allows women the opportunity to experience orgasm *i.e.* reaching sexual peak pleasure without any assistance of a partner to release sexual tension.

5. What if parents find their child Masturbating?

Ans. Parents should simply ignore this act of Masturbation of their child and not get their child scolded. Parents are adviced to simply brief their wards about private and public exposures of sex and allied activities.

6. How males and females perform Masturbation?

Ans. Females perform Masturbation by massaging the clitoris with hands and fingers or rubbing the vulva up against pillow, bed cloths, teddy beers or even with furniture parts. Apart from clitoral eroticism, vaginal panetration with the help of some slender fruits or inamimate object has also been in practice. Artificial penis called vibrator or dildo are available, commercially. Inserting a vibrator into vagina can help locate and stimulate the G-spot and offer a feeling of fullness of vagina. For good excitation and enjoyment even nipple can be stimulated.

Males stroke to reach orgasm while making to and fro movements over shaft of penis with bare hands or with some clothing with or without a lubricant, in the act of masturbation.

7. Does a good frequency of Masturbation reduce the thickness or length of penis?

Ans. No, never.

Laughter and sex are powerful antidote to mental as well as physical stress.

8. Does Gratification of Masturbation is same as actual coitus?

Ans. Theoretically no. It all depends upon the attention of subject. Actual coitus is an act of long duration with emotional as well as physical involvement of two different bodies, trying to reach Himalayan peaks of excitement and orgasm finally. As stated earlier, Masturbation is a solo act having superficial and short duration involvement to find orgasm. Many times it is a routine and compulsion act for males to get rid of frustration, abstinence or exhaustion (pain) or routine of life. The Masturbation can be enjoyed as good as coitus while even actual coitus may turn out to be just a phasic Masturbation.

9. What is the difference between Masturbation and Night fall or wet dreams (Nocturnal Ejaculation)?

Ans. Masturbation is known as a voluntary act being regulated by orientation and intelligence. Wet dreams are involuntary act of ejaculation during sleep because of accumulated sexual tension. Females also dream in the similar way to reach orgasm involuntarily, but there is no phase of ejaculation as it is there with males.

10. Can Masturbation be advisable to youngsters?

Ans. Yes, because it helps:

a. In maintaining physical and mental health.

b. As youngsters can recognise and control their sexual responses.

c. In maintaining better relationships between school/ college going teenagers and young adults, by this solo act.

d. Females who don't reach orgasm through coitus can receive pleasure through Masturbation.

e. Relieve anxiety and tension while one of partner is ill or on tour or in menses or in late pregnancy or immediately after child-birth.

Do not haste with act of sex. Haste is good only in catching fleas.

f. Masturbation is not a disease but voluntary outlet of sexual desires. To act as pleasurable safety valve which can avoid unwanted pregnancies and sexually transmitted infections both in Bachelors and spinsters and married couples also.

g. In keeping the sexual crime in society at low level.

If one can do, then why ask about myth and facts, just do it to help yourself one.

Oral Sex (Oro Genital Sex)

It is also known as Connilingus/fellatio. It is defined as penetration or licking of penis into oral cavity or licking with tongue the vestibule or the area around it. The technique for this type of sex activity include kissing, licking, sucking and friction of penis inside the woman's oral cavity.

Oral sex is completely healthy provided both the participants are approving it. This natural activity of oral sex is most delightful aspect of love and immensely satisfying to both the partners. Oral sex has 2 phases as fellatio and connilingus. Fellatio is kissing and sucking of male organ penis while connilingus is kissing and licking of vagina and vulva with the help of tongue and lips. Oral sex is also known as mouth music, a relatively easy technique to master, to approach orgasm, in a fairly short span of time. Swallowing vaginal or seminal fluids is harmless, except in pregnancy.

Connilingus

In connilingus a man uses his mouth to stimulate a woman's genitals.

To start having mouth generated music, anticipate a magical music of strings that is going to ring in the females brain. After stimulation of body's different part, concentrate on vaginal area. Try to bend down and place few dry kisses first and then wet kisses around the vulva. Sensitive males can catch-hold of shiver and muscular contraction, females go through with their thigh region and with a sigh-ecstasy from their mouth. Males

---

Foreplay can be assisted with music, light, food, drinks, dance and flowers.

should gently move their lips an inch or two downwards, until in the area of clitoris. An enthusiastic reaction from females, gets the male, a hint that they are in right spot at clitoris. Here in this area tongue should be moved back and forth over the clitoris. This procedure can be improvised to actually push the tongue into the vagina and moving it rapidly in and out. This is a highly effective method of stimulation, enjoyed by most women. Breathing difficulty, sometimes arises with males which with span of time can very easily be learnt while doing connilingus.

Fellatio

In fellatio, a woman uses her mouth to stimulate male's genitals.

It is needed to have good hygiene at the tip of the penis and under cover of glans part of penis. Here again reaching directly or kissing or sucking the penis is not appropriate as well as a welcome thing. Commence to kiss the neck, his chest, his nipples, arms, stomach and umbilicus. If a female has never had any kind of oral sex, she can very easily be adviced to begin with holding the penis and applying kiss after kiss to the tip or glans part of penis. Kissing will definitely facilitate taking the tip in the mouth and rocking gently forwards and backwards. Two risks present with fellatio are :

1. Depth of penetration and possible choking of throat.
2. Possibility of ejaculation.

For penetration, males can get directed from the beginning to understand the female's feeling too, as male approaches female's mouth in just the same way as he does enter the vagina. Ejaculation in mouth have mixed responses of hate and happiness. The ejaculate (semen/fluid) actually is completely harmless even when it is swallowed, except in pregnancy.

Two way oral sex mimics 69 position as both partners have their heads between each other's thigh. Half of 69 is 34½, which is most enjoyed posture by the couples.

6

Guide to Safer Sex

Playing safe sex is necessary for physical, mental, social and spiritual health of individual and society both.

Safe sex practice is essential for the following benefits :

1. Prevention of unwanted babies.
2. Prevention of sexually transmitted diseases.
3. Prevention of social sexual hatred.
4. Prevention of post-sex act guilt and tension.
5. Helps in maintaining a sound mental health.
6. Help to prepare the young generation to learn about safe pleasure.

Safe Sex to Prevent Diseases

W.H.O. has stressed since 1980, a lot on safe sex to prevent diseases because of advent of AIDS. The most important factor here is multiple partners. (1) By profession (2) By exchange or (3) For a change.

Safe sex is any sexual activity that does not involve penetration or exchange of body fluids and therefore it is considered risk free.

The best protection is to choose sexual activities that do not allow semen, vaginal fluid or blood to enter vagina, male urethral opening, mouth or anal opening or even skin where it has an open cut or sore.

These fluids can carry the HIV, which causes AIDS.

Specific Safer Sex Practice include:

1. A mutually faithful relationship between two uninfected partners.
2. Using a condom for all types of intercourse—i.e. vaginal, anal and oral.
3. Non-penetrative sex practices such as hugging, kissing, rubbing and masturbating.
4. Reducing the number of sexual partners.
5. Avoiding sex when you have open sores or any sexually transmitted disease (STD).
6. Avoiding sex with partners who have open sores or STDs.

Multiplicity has led to spread of S.T.D. by many folds. Some of common sexually transmitted diseases are:

1. Syphilis
2. Gonorrhoea
3. Chancroid
4. Lympho-Granuloma Venereum (LGV)
5. Herpes Zoster and H. Simplex
6. Trichomoniasis
7. Non-Gonococcal Urethritis (NGU)
8. Genital warts
9. Viral Hepatitis
10. Bacterial vaginosis
11. Candidiasis
12. Scabies
13. AIDS (HIV)

Unprotected Sex

Unprotected sex is the basic reason of spread of STDs in sex partners.

Sex is like enjoyable journey and destination is just exhaustion.

For STDs also, prevention is always better than cure. The methods of prophylaxis are as under:

1. Educational Awareness
2. Social Behaviour
3. Personal Behaviour
4. Chemotherapeutics.

Mass media communication for educational awareness is one of the most diversified way to reach even at grossroot level. Behavioural improvement at society and personal level with correct sex education facilitate hidden and exposed prophylaxis from the STDs. Use of condom is the most important and effective way for STD prevention.

The methods of STD prophylaxis are listed below as:

a. Use condom during Intercourse.
b. Abstinence.
c. Establishment of a monogamous relationship with an uninfected sexual partner.
d. Unprotected post-exposure antibiotic oriented systemic prophylaxis.

So if you want to be safe:

1. Be careful with your choice of Partner.
2. Avoid anything intimate until you are ready to commit yourself to him or her.
3. Use Barriers, if possible along with spermicides and use them all the time.

How Condoms are Used

Condom was a name of a village in France where people used to wear a rubber cap over the penis to prevent pregnancy. Commonly available as *Nirodh*, in India, the condoms are made of Latex which is good in tensile strength and is elastic. Condom fits over the erect penis acting as barrier in transmission of semen into vagina. Condom by standard is about 19 cm. long and 2.5 cm. wide. Condom is beneficial for the following reasons:

1. Prevents pregnancy.
2. Prevents STDs and AIDS.

3. Enhance pleasure by delaying man's orgasm (pre-mature ejaculation).
4. Handy to carry over in pocket without any exposure, easily.
5. Quick to use to have safe sex.
6. Flavoured, smooth, dotted and lubricated condoms enhance pleasure of sex.
7. More acceptable in use and self-explanatory.

Risks about Condom

1. May get ruptured while intercourse is performed.
2. In extreme arousal, this latex can easily be forgotten, to be worn.
3. Sensitivity reaction to condom.
4. Never re-use a condom.
5. Never use oil based lubricants. Lubricants such as vaseline, hand lotion or massage oil weaken the latex and may make condom break. If needed water based lubricants can be used.

Precautions for Use of Condoms

1. Thick skinned condom is a greater safety against spillage and rupture.
2. Condom with a sperm killing cream facilitate superior safety to prevent a pregnancy.
3. Cylinder of condom should have the reservoir at the tip to accommodate and store the ejaculate.
4. Go for tested and standardized condoms of established brands, which can bear extremes of stress and devoid of any puncture.
5. Condom should be worn in the initial stages of erection to prevent STD and pregnancy. Many of the times the initial discharge of cowper's gland to lubricate the tip of glans of penis might have some active and motile sperms

reaching uterine cavity and fallopian tube, where it may join OVUM and conceive a baby.

6. While wearing the condom, it is advised to deflate the air, present at the tip (reservoir of condom).
7. Condom withdrawal after ejaculation should be done with utmost care with holding of the rim so that no spillage take place in or around vulva while penis is being withdrawn.
8. Condoms are used always one at a time and after single use they should be destroyed. For every sexual act a new condom be used.

How to Put on a Condom

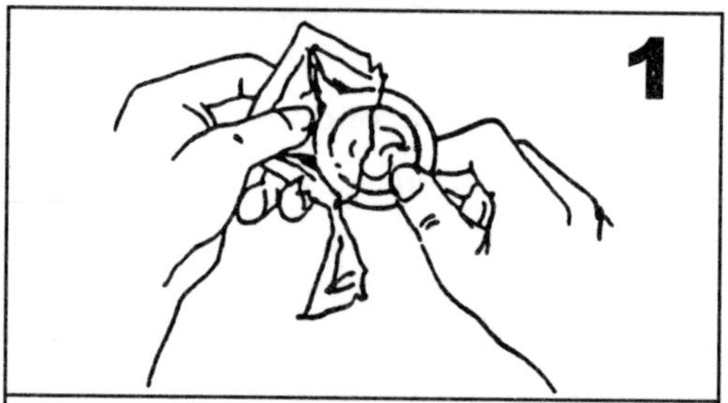

Carefully open package so condom does not tear. Do not unroll condom before putting it on.

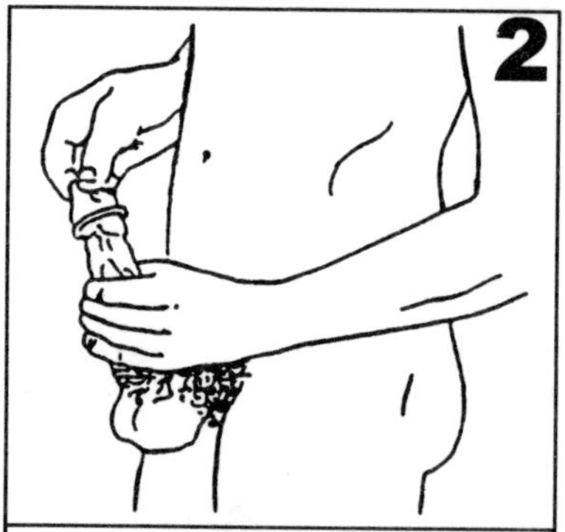

If not circumcised, pull foreskin back. Squeeze tip of condom and put it on end of hard penis.

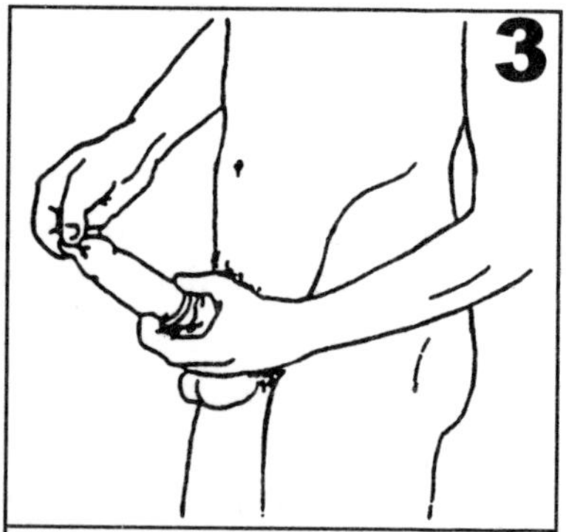

Continue squeezing tip while unrolling condom until it covers all of penis.

Never Re-use a condom.

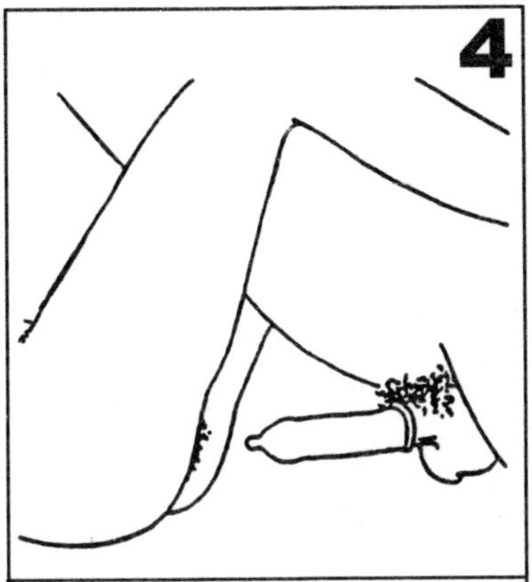

Always put condom on before entering partner.

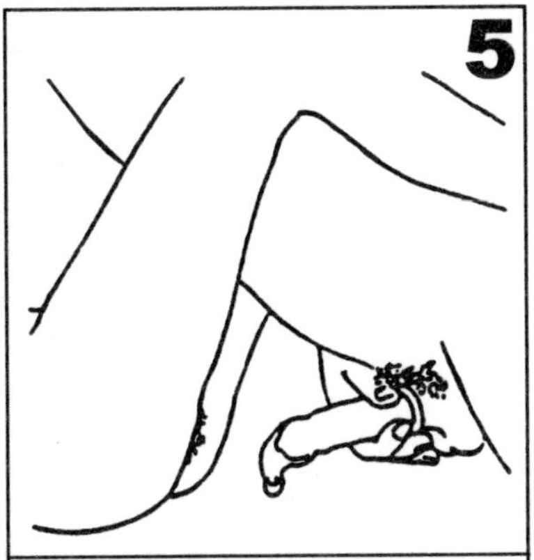

After ejaculating (coming), hold rim of condom and pull penis out before penis gets soft.

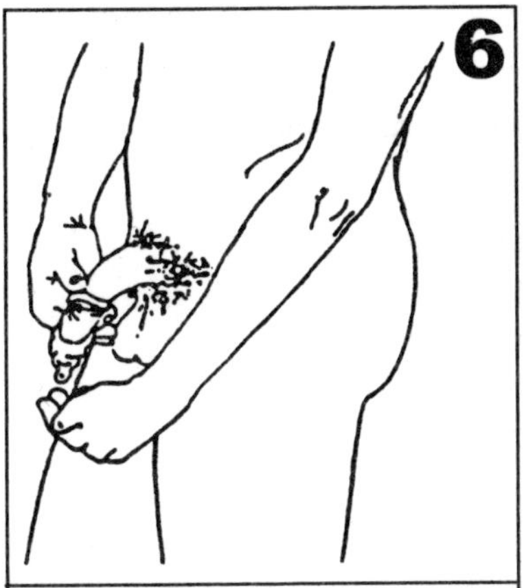

Slide condom off without spilling liquid (semen) inside.

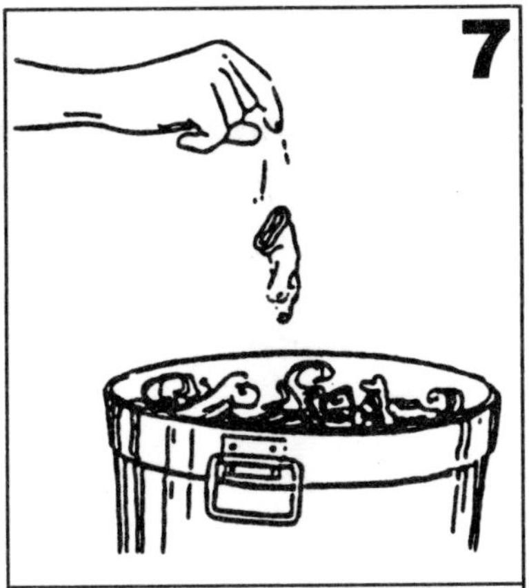

Throw away or bury the condom. Do not flush the discarded condom.

Remember

- Do not use grease, oils, lotions, or petroleum jelly (Vaseline) to make condoms slippery. These make condoms break. Only use a jelly or cream that does not have oil in it.
- Use a condom each time you have sex.
- Only use a condom once.
- Store condoms in a cool, dry place.
- Do not use condoms that may be old or damaged.

  Do not use a condom if:

  – the package is broken

  – the condom is brittle or dried out

  – the color is uneven or changed—it is unusually sticky.

Three Rules to Safeguard Character

1. Rule of thinking twice, before any commitment.
2. Rule of Denial, before any surrender.
3. Rule of understanding the Hidden Agenda behind the Gift/offer.

Teenage girls should be trained to identify possibility of physical exploitation.

7

Foreplay

The act of sexual intercourse is not just penetration of penis into vagina and reaching orgasm. Orgasm is final destination of the journey of act of sex which is comprised of various stages as under before actual intercourse is done.

1. Verbal communication.
2. Touching the body with
   - Hugging
   - Stroking
   - Petting
   - Cuddling
   - Embracing
3. Kissing at different sensitive parts of body.
4. Massaging and caressing.

Fundamental Points of Foreplay

1. Partners need to be free with each other about what they are going to enjoy during foreplay.
2. Undressing has its own enjoyment
   - by self or by partner.
   - in dark or in illuminated room.
   - in closed room or in open space as in garden or at sea-beach.

Nervi erigentis are group of nerves responsible for Erection.

- by consent or against little resistance.
- with slow pace or rapid speed of undressing.

3. To get an emotional touch in sex, foreplay is must and to prevent creeping in of mechanics factor of routine in sex.
4. Touch is the universally accepted feeling of gratification through fingertips stroking at
   - The back and flanks.
   - Nipples of breasts.
   - Soft and tender lips.
   - Around vulva.
   - At the clitoris.
5. Soft massage with the fist or open palm facilitate a gentle cruise of the partner's desire towards orgasm. Soft tissue massage of the following is very helpful in the very sequence of:
   - Back and flanks.
   - Buttocks.
   - Breasts.
   - Thighs.

   The act of soft tissue massage is not only good as recreation but also for refreshment from the tired day long activities. The blood supplies in the massaged area is increased leading to faster metabolism and drainage of waste products resulting in pain relief and getting your partner afresh. This massage phenomenon is good for both men and women. Man also likes to be touched and to be stroked on the sensitive parts of back and belly and buttocks. To have his penis caressed, either cradled in the palm of his wife/girl friend's hand or manipulated with gentle fingers, gets man to enjoyable peaks without reaching orgasm.
6. *Exclusive genital massage:* In this process, man on top or woman on top, gently caress their respective genitals

against each other without having any help of hands or fingers. Here the tip and shaft of penis act as an active, thick finger to stimulate the vulva, by rubbing against clitoris, and vaginal opening. In return the penis also is caressed passively to feel for unforgettable moments of pleasure.

7. Foreplay gives feeling of assurance and security apart from pleasure. Foreplay is a sense of giving and sharing which gets the partner rid of anxiety, frustration and fear about sex which he/she might be having since his/her childhood.
8. Good foreplay helps reaching the orgasm in both the partners. This attainment of orgasm together gives immense sexual satisfaction. This physical and the emotional satisfaction is well integrated. This is total relationship.
9. Marriage has 3 ingredients namely LAF i.e. Love, Acceptance and Freedom. The fun of life can be approached with L.A.F. which is generated at the act of sex. Foreplay before sex helps you and your partner to build up 3 stairs of Love, Acceptance and Freedom. The closeness, foreplay helps to reach bring companionship and belongingness for being appreciated, wanted and understood.
10. Physically, foreplay helps stimulate the Erogenous zone males and females have at different parts of body as in and around:
    - Lips.
    - Breast.
    - Back.
    - Flanks.
    - Buttocks.
    - Thigh.
    - Genitals.

Multiple orgasm is possible in female in even a single act.

11. Foreplay can be assisted by sensation play. Above all 3 most important elements to become a better lover are:
    1. Learning to feel.
    2. Choosing what pleases you and your partner.
    3. Empathy.

    "Sensation play" consists of following components:
    - Spanking.
    - Scratching.
    - Pinching.
    - Hair Pulling.
    - Hugging.
    - Teasing.

While practising these things sympathy, empathy and good security measures should always be taken care of as your partner may get injured physically and emotionally.

8

Erotic Massage and Sex Deviations

The idea of erotic massage, as the name itself suggests is to bring your partner to high levels of arousal and keep him or her there for some time. Erotic massage has a provider and receiver and vice versa. Like a partner to receive a massage first and then to return the favour.

Erotic massage is started with a sensual and relaxing general massage before shifting the erroneous focus to your partner's sex centres.

Erotic massage is done:

1. In man through verbal or non-verbal communication which allows stimulation to be slowed down, changed or stopped before ejaculation is inevitable.
2. In woman through using G-spot stimulation massage or clitoral massage to bring her to multiple orgasms.

Delayed love making and Orgasm

- Desensitize the penis:
  - Wearing double condom
  - Pull out to break the continuity of thrusting into the vagina
- Try different positions:
- **Kegel's Exercise:** Human body is a structure of Bones and Muscles. Out of 640 odd muscles, one muscle is known for

Females with excessive non-satiable sex desires are called NYMPHOMANIACS.

enhancement in sexual gratification. This muscle is identified as to function to stop the flow of urine while one urinates. A regular pattern of exercising the contraction and relaxation of this muscle will lead to development of holding of ejaculation for quite some time. This is Kegel's exercise. A continuous contraction of pubococcygeus (PC) muscle while inhaling and relaxing the muscle while exhaling, in the free time shall definitely enhance the performance in bed.

This sex potentiating exercise can be performed anywhere at anytime till the subject is stationary.

The benefits of Kegel's Exercise are as follows:

For Women	*For Men*
• Easy to reach climax	• Stronger Erection
• Intense Orgasm	• Intense Orgasm
• Enhanced Sensitivity in and around vaginal orifice	• Reduced risk of impotence
• Easier child-birth	

Sex Deviations

Sex is a gender thing i.e. either it is male or female, while sexuality of a person is either Straight or Gay or Bisexual. It does mean that sexual attraction is towards opposite sex as being Straight, while Gay or Lesbianism is to designate sexual inclination of attraction towards same sex i.e. Males and females respectively.

The Bisexual is a person who has a psyche of attraction to both males and females. The deviations of sexual psyche can be:

(a) **Homosexuality** – Receiving sexual gratification from same sex partner.

(b) **Sadism** – Sexual gratification by inflicting pain to the partner.

(c) **Masochism** – Sexual gratification by receiving painful stimulus from the partner.

Ejaculation is delayed in grown age so also resolution.

(d) **Fetishism** – Sexual gratification with the foul smell of faeces etc.

(e) **Exhibitionism** – Sexual gratification by exhibiting whole body or part of body in public.

(f) **Voyeurism** – This means enjoying while seeing how an actual act is taking place.

(g) **Transvestism** – Sexual gratification by dressing up with opposite sex's garments.

(h) **Pedophilia** – This abnormal sexual behaviour is to have sexual relations with young children.

(i) **Bestiality** – Establishing sex with the animals.

Intercourse is highly volatile activity practised as missionary, quickie etc.

9

Anal/Rectal Sex

Penetration of penis into the anal opening down to anal canal and rectum is rectal sex/intercourse.

This practice is pretty common and it is said that about 20-30% of married couples have tried this practice at some time or other in their sex life.

Conditions facilitating urge for rear entry are:

1. Pregnancy.
2. Vaginal Infections.
3. Menstrual Discharge.
4. Vaginismus.
5. Deviation from routine vaginal sex.
6. Simultaneous fondling of female breasts.

Anal sex is basically harmless, opposite to common belief and is an enjoyable as long as both of the partners can relish it. Many of the times, a normal vaginal delivery of a child loosens the vaginal tube and this changes the eroticism and feel of orgasm differently while forward and backward movements of penis are made in the vagina.

Apart from anal intercourse, anal stimulation has also been enjoyed by couples. The anus is quite sensitive to touch and many women enjoy stimulation of this area during masturbation or during intercourse. This is highly erogenous area and can be stimulated with the finger or with anal toys namely anal beads and anal dildos or butt plugs.

Anus and Rectum Anatomy

The main function of rectum to act as a storage unit for stools/ faeces and small amount may remain always in the rectum. That is why it is always advised to use condoms during anal intercourse. The rectum is not straight between the anal opening and rectum and in between is present anal canal. The lining of rectum is very thin and can rip off if too much of stress is put on it. The control of anal opening is regulated voluntarily by central nervous system. The internal sphincter of anal canal and rectum is being regulated involuntarily by autonomic nervous system. The internal sphincter reflects and responds to fear and anxiety.

Misconceptions about Anal Sex

Q. It is always an uncomfortable experience?

Ans. This is false.

Q. First few anal insertions are painful?

Ans. Yes, it is true for vaginal intercourse also. It always need some practice to get accustomed to the activity. Pain with anal sex is usually a sign that the act is being performed incorrectly.

Q. Anal sex is full of pain because of fast and hard entry?

Ans. Yes, it is true to some extent. The pain in most cases is due to following reasons :

1. Receiver's anxiety.
2. Receiver's tightening of muscles.
3. Rear entry by penis is too hard.
4. Penis size is too big.
5. Not enough lubricant.

Medications help erection but not sustenance of erection.

Q. What guidelines should be followed for anal intercourse?

Ans. Six point major guidelines are:

a. Good use of water based lubricants which are latex compatible, are always recommended for easy and painless entry and enjoyment.

b. Stop immediately if the partner asks to stop. The anxiety and tense posture of partner may hurt or torn the anal opening or soft and tender mucosa (lining) of anal canal and rectum.

c. Go slow. Slow and steady propagation through the passage will definitely get the partner relaxed to build a positive acceptance and generation of desire for insertion of penis.

d. Positive and continuous communication with the partner, builds enough faith in the male partner by female.

e. Be open about the preferences and feelings of the partner and be respective to partner.

f. It is must to have stimulation of anal opening with tender finger tip, tongue tip or penis tip to generate giving feeling in and around the anal opening. Before the entry of penis is made, it is always recommended to insert little finger tip through anus to get the opening ready for still large hardened and thickened penis with appropriate lubricant.

NB. Anal intercourse is good for a changed feel of orgasm, but it is to be remembered for anal sex or any other variation in sex, that, enter where, where your entry is welcome.

Stress in sex will distress you, by taking away your performance.

10

STD/STI

WHO reports that there are 250 million new cases of sexually transmitted diseases/infections reported every year, of which one million are HIV infections. In terms of productive healthy life years lost STDs are estimated to be second only to water borne diseases in their burden upon human health. Yet STD prevention and treatment has not been a priority, because of:

1. Social Taboo.
2. Absent Symptoms.
3. Social beliefs that STDs do not cause morbidity and mortality.
4. Illiteracy.
5. Poverty.

STDs have significant causes of morbidity and mortality for centuries and every day thousands of new cases are added to the list. If STDs are left untreated they can result in:

1. Pelvic Inflammatory disease.
2. Infertility.
3. Urethral stricture.
4. Ectopic Pregnancy.
5. Cervical Cancer.
6. Congenital Syphilis.
7. Infant Blindness.

8. Mental Retardation.
9. Still birth.
10. Miscarriage.
11. Death.

One of the most dreaded and fatal STD is AIDS, also known as SLIM Disease. AIDS is caused by a virus which breaks down the Body's defence/immune system. AIDS is now considered a pandemic, affecting developed, developing and poor countries alike.

STDs are presented with the following common symptoms:

a. Genital Ulcer (male + female)
b. Urethral Discharge (male)
c. Vaginal Discharge (female)
d. Lower Abdominal pain (female)

a. Genital ulcers are seen with following STDs:

1. Syphilis.
2. Chancroid.

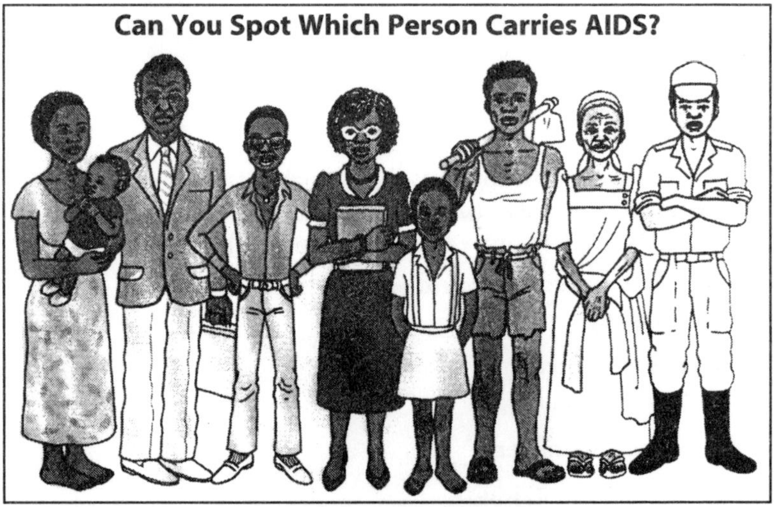

Fig. 10.1: The Answer in NO! The virus causing AIDS can hide in blood for years together.

The biggest way to catch AIDS is sexual acts.

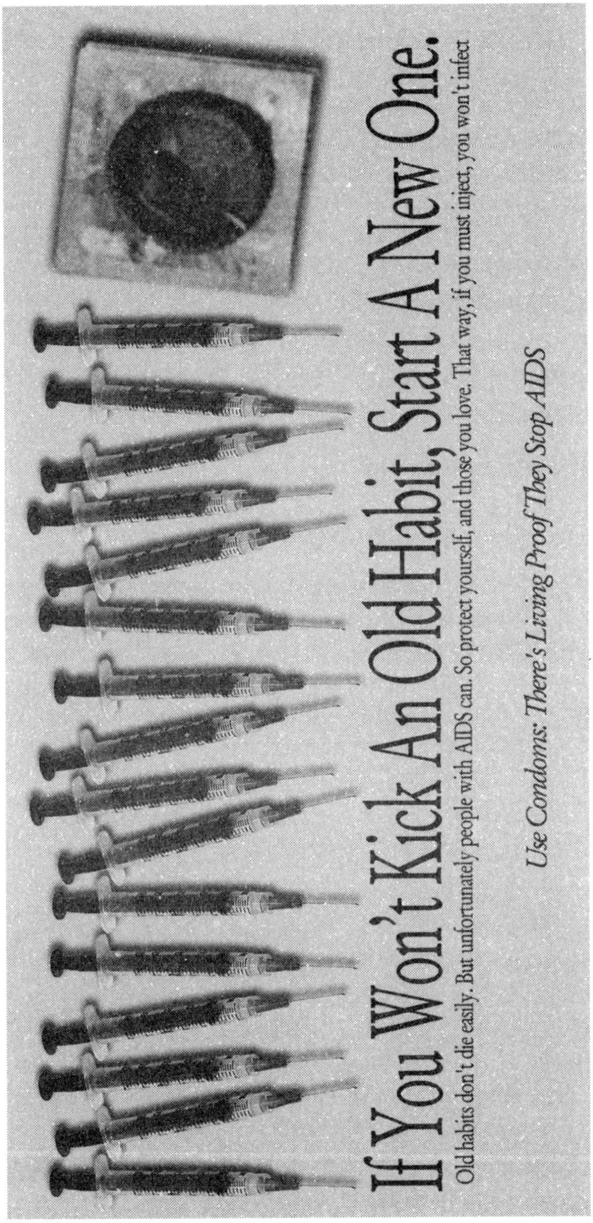

Fig. 10.2: Stop Injectiny Drug Abuse and Unsafe Sex.

3. Herpes.
4. L.G.V.
5. Donovanosis.

b. Urethral Discharge:

1. Gonorrhoea.
2. Chlamydia.

c. Vaginal Discharge:

1. Gonorrhoea.
2. Chlamydia.
3. Trichomoniasis.
4. Bacterial Vaginosis.

d. Lower Abdominal Pain

Pelvic Inflammatory disease which can be a result of any of above mentioned STD/STIs.

STDs are diseases caused and communicated primarily by sexual contact. Many variety of micro-organisms are transmitted through sex from one partner to another. The table below specifically mention the names of bacteria/virus involved with STDs:

Sl.No.	*Name of STD*	*Name of Organism*
1.	Syphilis	Treponema Pallidum
2.	Gonorrhoea	Neisseria gonorrhoeae
3.	Chancroid	Hemophilus ducreyi
4.	Herpes	Herpes simplex virus 1 or 2
5.	LGV	Chlamydia trachomatis
6.	Donovanosis	Calymmato bacterium granulomatis
7.	Chlamydia	Chlamydia trachomatis
8.	Candidiasis	Candida albicans (fungus)
9.	Trichomoniasis	Trichomonia
10.	AIDS	Human Immuno-deficiency Virus (HIV)

Love is giving your entire self without expecting anything in return.

Fig. 10.3: Various Placards showing methods to stop sexual transmission of H.I.V.

Non-Notifiable Infections are:

1. Genital Warts — virus
2. Genital Herpes — Herpes virus
3. Molluscum Contagiosum — virus
4. Candidosis (Moniliasis) — fungus
5. Trichomoniasis — Bacteria
6. Infestations like scabies (Parasite)
7. NGU — Non gonococcal urethritis.

AIDS / HIV is transmitted by the following 8 ways:

1. Unprotected sexual contact with an infected person. Homo or Heterosexually.
2. Transfusion of blood and blood products.
3. Sharing of common needle or syringes by drug abusers.
4. Perinatally from infected mother to child.
5. Infected mother to the infant via breast milk.
6. Tattooing, ear piercing and acupuncture.
7. Organ transplants or surgeries from HIV positive patient.
8. Infected semen in procedure of artificial insemination (A.I.) in infertile couple.

The HIV is transmitted in semen, cervical, vaginal fluid and in blood or blood products. In an infected person, these fluids are rich in AIDS virus along with cerebrospinal fluid. Other body fluids such as tears, saliva and sweat contain few HIV infected cells, therefore very rarely account for transmission.

Now question arise is that what sexual activities are safe, probably safe and very unsafe to understand prevention measures from STDs.

Safe Sexual Activities for AIDS:

Where no exchange of semen, blood or vaginal secretions take place:

1. Hugging.

Female condoms are an alternative to male condoms for vaginal intercourse and equally good for Anal intercourse.

Fig. 10.4: Follow the rule of thinking twice before you say-yes

2. Touching.
3. Massage.
4. Rubbing the bodies together.
5. Talking about sex.
6. Kissing or licking the clean skin of body with no oral contact with genitals or any open wound, ulcer or sore.

The actual site of sex is not between the Thighs, but between the ears, i.e. in Brain.

7. Masturbation by self or by partner.

Unsafe Sexual Activities for AIDS

1. Vaginal intercourse without a condom.
2. Oral intercourse without a condom.
3. Anal intercourse without a condom.
4. Activity allowing blood to blood contact.
5. Activity allowing contact of semen/vaginal secretions with mucous membrane at oral cavity/nasal cavity/ vaginal cavity or at anal canal.
6. Sharing objects being inserted into the vagina or anus.

Probably Safe Sexual Practices for AIDS

1. Vaginal intercourse with proper use of intact condom.
2. Oral intercourse with proper use of intact condom.
3. Anal intercourse with proper use of intact condom.
4. French kissing i.e. wet kiss of mouth to mouth, provided kiss does not draw blood or there is no open sore/ulcer in or around the mouth.
5. Masturbation with hands, by partner provided no contact of vagina or oral cavity or anus is being made in extreme excitement.

STDs along with HIV or AIDS can be avoided by following universal measures:

1. Maintaining mutual and faithful relationship with your spouse (husband or wife).
2. Use of a condom while establishing sex vaginally, orally or anally with a partner you are not certain.
3. Accept blood transfusion only when absolutely necessary.
4. In case of essential blood transfusion proper testing for HIV should always be done, as a rule.
5. In case of elective surgery auto-transfusion of blood should be encouraged.

Never use an oil based lubricant on the condom.

6. HIV positive women should be on good contraceptives to avoid pregnancy.
7. Use always properly sterilized or disposable needle and syringe in Intramuscular, Intravenous or Subcutaneous injections.
8. Never allow sharing or exchange of syringes, for injecting drugs/fluids.
9. Avoid being tattooed as needles used in tottooing may be infected.
10. Cosmetic skin piercing of any type like Ear-piercing, acupuncture or scarification to be done by properly sterilized instruments.

The reported or diagnosed cases of AIDS just represent tip of the Iceberg. Being affected with the AIDS virus, HIV is not the same as having AIDS. Many people who carry the virus do so unknowingly, without any presentation of symptoms. HIV carriers suffer intermediate illness namely PGL and ARC.

N.B. PGL — Persistent Generalized Lymphadenopathy.

ARC — AIDS Related Complications.

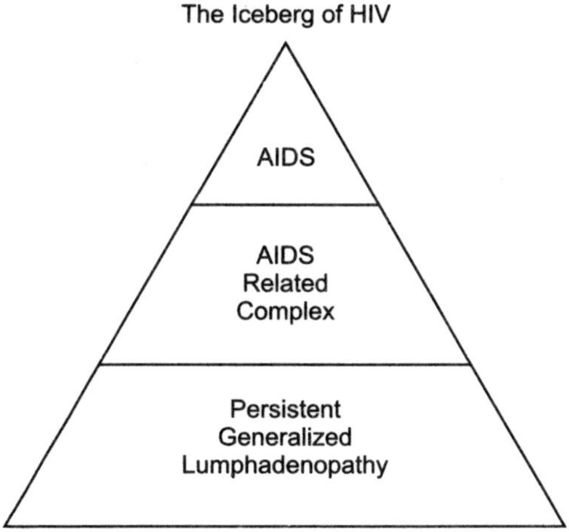

Fig. 10.5: Iceberg of HIV/AIDS.

HIV Infection

The high risk group for AIDS are:

1. Drug abusers with needle sharing.
2. Prostitutes, or CSW (Community Sex Workers)
3. Males, regularly going to prostitute.
4. Male Homosexuals.
5. Anal Intercourse.
6. Promiscuous male/female with multiple sexual partners.
7. Person receiving repeated blood transfusion.
8. Person going for organ transplantation.
9. Person going for regular hemolysis and peritoneal dialysis.
10. Person going for elective or emergency surgery.
11. Person with sexually transmitted infections, notifiable or non-notifiable.
12. Casual sex vaginally, anally or orally with strangers.
13. Intercourse with individuals known to be HIV-positive.
14. Avoid sex when you have open sores or any STD.
15. Avoid sex with partners who have open sores or STD.

Safe activities with which HIV is not transmitted from one person to another are:

- Living together.
- Holding hands.
- Kissing.
- Sport playing.
- Toilet seats.
- Touching.
- Dancing.
- Bathing together.
- Hugging.

Use the word "No". There is no good substitute to this, for teenagers, when somebody offers to have sex.

- Massage.
- Sharing food and utensils.
- Swimming.
- Sneezing.
- Coughing.
- Breathing.
- Sharing clothes.
- Sharing telephone.
- Travelling together.
- Working together.
- Bite of flies or Mosquito.

Probably safe or unsafe is:

- Sharing of Razor and
- Sharing of Tooth brush.

This Human-Immunodeficiency Virus when exposed in atmosphere is having just a life span of 3 seconds therefore the above mentioned activities are very safe.

Obviously prostitutes are at high risk for AIDS because they have many sexual partners. Both male and female prostitutes should be given and directed to follow these messages:

1. Use condoms with all partners every time you have sex.
2. Get STDs treated promptly.
3. Do not have sex with partners who have open sore.
4. Do not have sex if you have open sore.

N.B. Stopping sexual transmission of HIV, three basic messages are:

1. Keep to your partner.
2. Abstain from sex.
3. Use condom always.

Just two ways to get protected from STD/HIV and pregnancy are:
(a) Abstinence (b) Condom.

It is also noted semen contain higher concentration of virus than vaginal, oral or anal secretions. Therefore it appears AIDS/HIV is transmitted better from man to woman than from woman to man. Of three types of intercourse, anal intercourse is most likely to develop abrasions because of thinner and tender mucous membrane. Here from the virus can be absorbed easily in the circulation.

Epidemiological Risk factors for AIDS:

- Present or Past High Risk behaviour.
- Drug Injecting.
- Multiple Sex Partners.
- Male Homosexuals.
- Recent History of Genital ulcer.
- History of receiving unscreened blood.
- Sexual Abuse.
- History of use of unsterile Instruments for minor procedures like circumcision.

11

Condoms

Named after a village in France where people used to practice to prevent conception. Condom are made of

1. Latex with or without spermicidal agent.
2. Lamb intestine.

Condom is placed over the erect penis to prevent the sperms from entering the vagina.

Latex condoms can effectively protect against most STDs and AIDS. Condoms are less effective in preventing STDs which are having ulcers, namely Herpes simplex, Syphilis, Granuloma - Inguinale and LGV. These STDs may still be transmitted as condom may not prevent contact between body areas like Labia Majora or Testes where lesions are found and skin to skin contact is very much possible.

Advantages of Condom

1. Protection against pregnancy.
2. Protection against STDs.
3. Protection against AIDS.
4. Protection against Carcinoma of Cervix in females.
5. Easily Available.
6. Easy to Use.
7. Cheap method for protection.

Sex is the most talked about topic by all genders, among classmates, jobmates and like minded fellows.

8. Helps in planning of family.
9. Helps in treating premature ejaculation.

Disadvantages of Condoms

1. Some male/female may be allergic to latex material of condom.
2. Some may feel irritation due to condom.

Cautions Before Condoms Are Being Used

1. Check for expiry date of condom while it is purchased.
2. Condom is for single use only and should never be re-used.
3. Condom should be put on when penis is erect and before it comes into contact with vulva.
4. Condom should never be tested by blowing up or filling with water or so.
5. Never use lubricating condoms with oil based products as Mineral Oil, Vegetable Oil, Cooking Oil, Vaseline, Baby Oil, or Butter, as these products weaken the texture of latex/rubber.
6. Condoms can be lubricated with spermicidal preparations, saliva, glycerine or water based lubricants.
7. Condoms have a shelf life of 3 years and are stored in cool, dark and dry place, protected from Sunlight, heat and humidity.
8. Condom provide good but not perfect protection. For the greatest margin of safety condoms must be used correctly from start to finish with every act of intercourse. This requires both a ready supply of condoms and motivation and cooperation between sexual partners.
9. Choose good quality branded condoms.
10. Condoms are best for adolescent boys and girls getting started for their sexual activities.

Government of India through its National Family Planning Programme distributes 72 condoms per annum at "No" cost, so that you can say "Yes" to Nirodh.

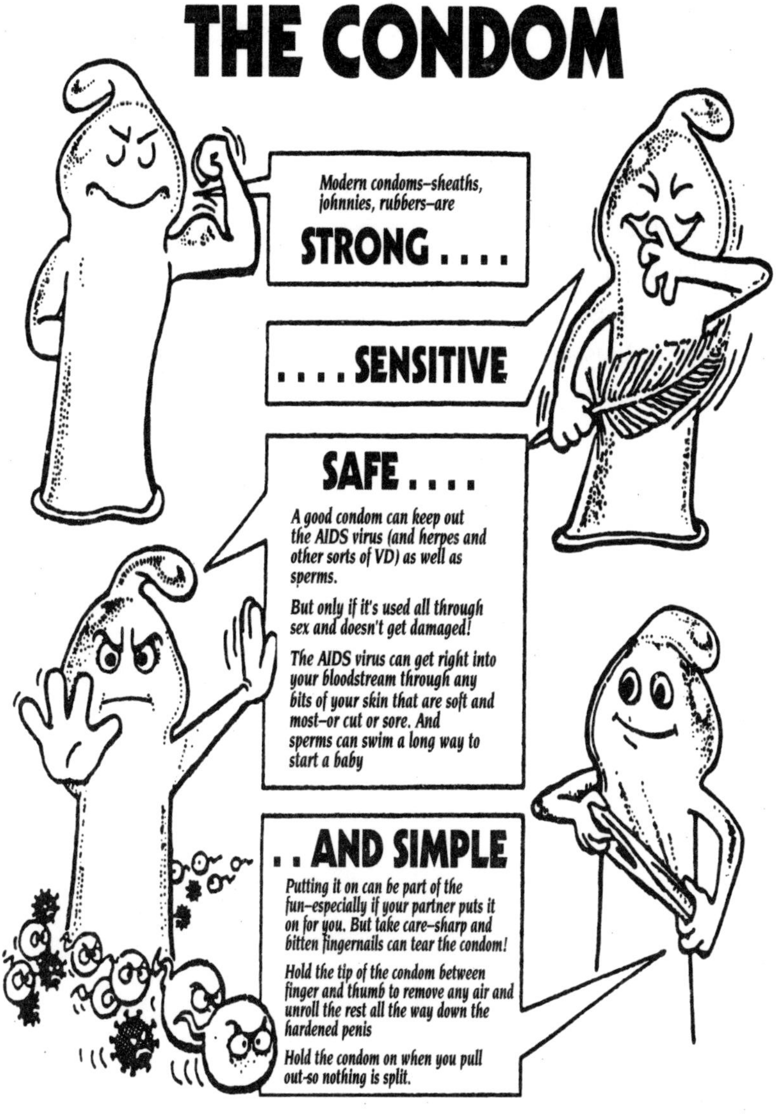

Abstain or remain faithful in sex relations as condoms provide good but not perfect protection.

Preventive Measures From S.T.D.

1. Be known and informed.
2. Be choosy.
3. Be cautious.
4. Be superviser.
5. Be tested.
6. Be treated.
7. Be faithful.
8. Be honest.
9. Be a Masturbationer.
10. Be condoman.

If he/she does not have a condom, you just have to take a deep breath and tell him to go get one.

12

Family Planning

Also known as "Birth Control", "Contraceptive methods" or fertility regulation methods.

Family planning is defined as the use of methods which help women avoid unwanted pregnancies. The described objectives of family planning are mentioned below:

1. To avoid unwanted births.
2. To bring about wanted births.
3. To keep the interval between pregnancies.
4. To manage the time at which births occur in relation to age of couple.
5. To determine the number of children in the family.

The family planning program advocates spacing between the birth of 2 children so that the first child gets his due love, Health, attention and care before he is 3 years old.

The family planning program also denounce pregnancy in rapid succession because of mother's health. Every pregnancy drains mother's reserve store of nutrients.

For family planning and contraception many a method are available, but the selection of contraceptive is influenced by the following basic measures:

1. Safety.

2. Efficacy.
3. Cultural and social taboos.
4. Factor of pleasure.
5. Acceptance by individual and public/society.
6. Known contraindications of method.

The contraceptive methods have been grouped into 2 broad classes:

A. Temporary or Reversible method.
B. Permanent or Terminal method.

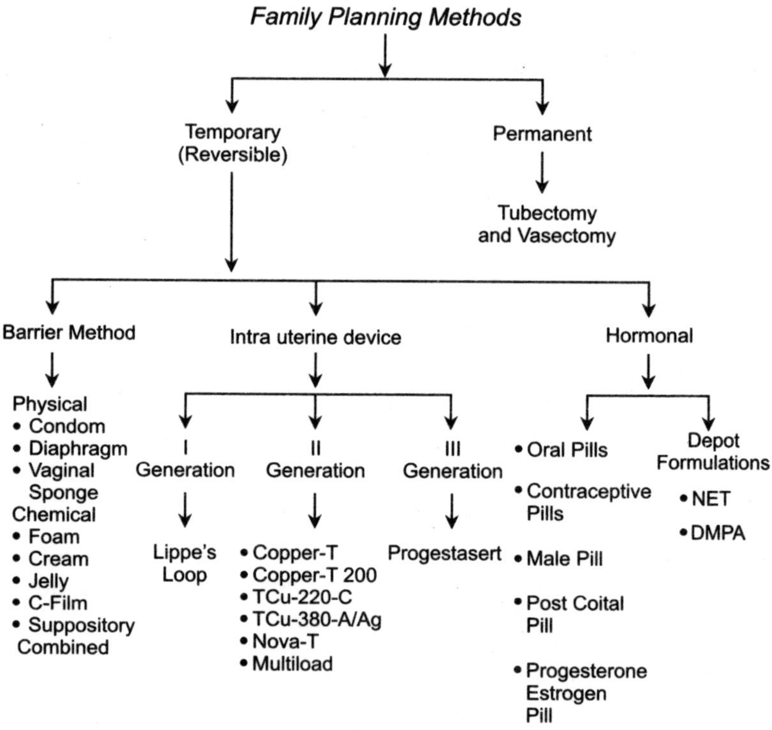

Communication (verbal-non verbal) is an integral part of any man-woman relationship.

Permanent Methods

Male sterilization

2 methods are used for vasectomy:

1. Routine vasectomy.
2. NSV i.e. No-scalpel vasectomy. In this method, no incision or cut is given to skin and no sutures are placed after crushing the vas deferens, which carry the sperms to ejaculate.

Female sterilization methods:

1. Laparoscopy (Abdominal).
2. Minilap surgery.

FAQ about contraceptive methods

Q.1. *Why to work on contraception?*

Ans. It is very important to talk with your partner about birth control before you have sexual intercourse and to get the facts to help you decide which methods are best for you and your partner. Awareness about birth control measures are necessary for following:

1. Inadvertent pregnancy.
2. Economical burden to family and nation.
3. Physical health of mother and child if spacing in short.
4. Fear of pregnancy curtails the factor of enjoyment or pleasure.
5. Morale and character of youth and society can be upheld.

Q.2. *Which method of family planning is best?*

Ans. It varies from person to person, situation to situation and from age to age and above all, of course, gender to gender. (See Q 4 and 5)

Do not use "I" but "we" to prevent your partner to become Bitter half from better half.

Q.3. What factors determine a contraceptive method to be chosen?

Ans. 1. Marital status.
2. Pleasure factor.
3. Character and morale.
4. Efficiency of method.
5. Past experience with a method.
6. Social influences.
7. Religious influences.
8. Age of user.
9. Disease status of user.
10. Smoking/Addiction/Drug dependence status of user.
11. Hazardous effect of method on user.
12. Short/long-term usage of method.

Q.4. According to Age, what method of contraception can be advocated as first and second choice?

Ans.

	Age	*1st Choice*	*2nd Choice*
1.	<19	Abstinence	Condom
2.	20-30 (Unmarried)	Condom	Combined pills
3.	20-30 (Married)	Combined pills	IUCD
4.	30-35 (Unmarried)	Condom	Combined pills
5.	30-35 (Married)	Combined pills	Condom
6.	35-50	Condom	IUCD

Q.5. According to profession, what methods of contraception can be advocated?

Ans.

	Profession	*1st choice*	*2nd choice*
1.	Housewife	Combined pills	IUCD
2.	Executives with promiscuity	Condom	Condom
3.	Student (Male + Female)	Abstinence	Condom
4.	Prostitute	Condom	Condom
5.	Professionals with promiscuity	Condom	Abstinence

Sexuality is our gender as Male/female and sexual orientation is as straight, Gay or Bisexual.

Q.6. According to Efficacy, how various contraceptive devices and methods be rated for protection against pregnancy and STD/HIV?

Ans.

	Contracaptive Method	*Efficacy (%) for Pregnancy*	*Efficacy (%) for STD/HIV*
1.	Abstinence	100%	100%
2.	Coitus interruptus	75-96%	00%
3.	Condom	86-97%	99%
4.	Pills (OCD)	95-98%	00%
5.	IUCD	99%	00%
6.	Injectables	99%	00%
7.	Physiological method		
	BBT	65-85%	00%
	CMM	78-80%	00%
	Calendar method (Fertility Awareness)	65-85%	00%
8.	VT/TT	100%	00%
9.	Post Conceptional method	100%	00%
10.	Chemical Barrier		
	Diaphragm	80-94%	—
	Cervical cap	80-91%	—
	Female condom	80-95%	95%
11.	Foam/Cream/Jelly/ Film/Suppository	74-95%	—

"Quickei" is quick intercourse in elevators, subway, in park or in bathroom, lasting for few seconds to few minutes.

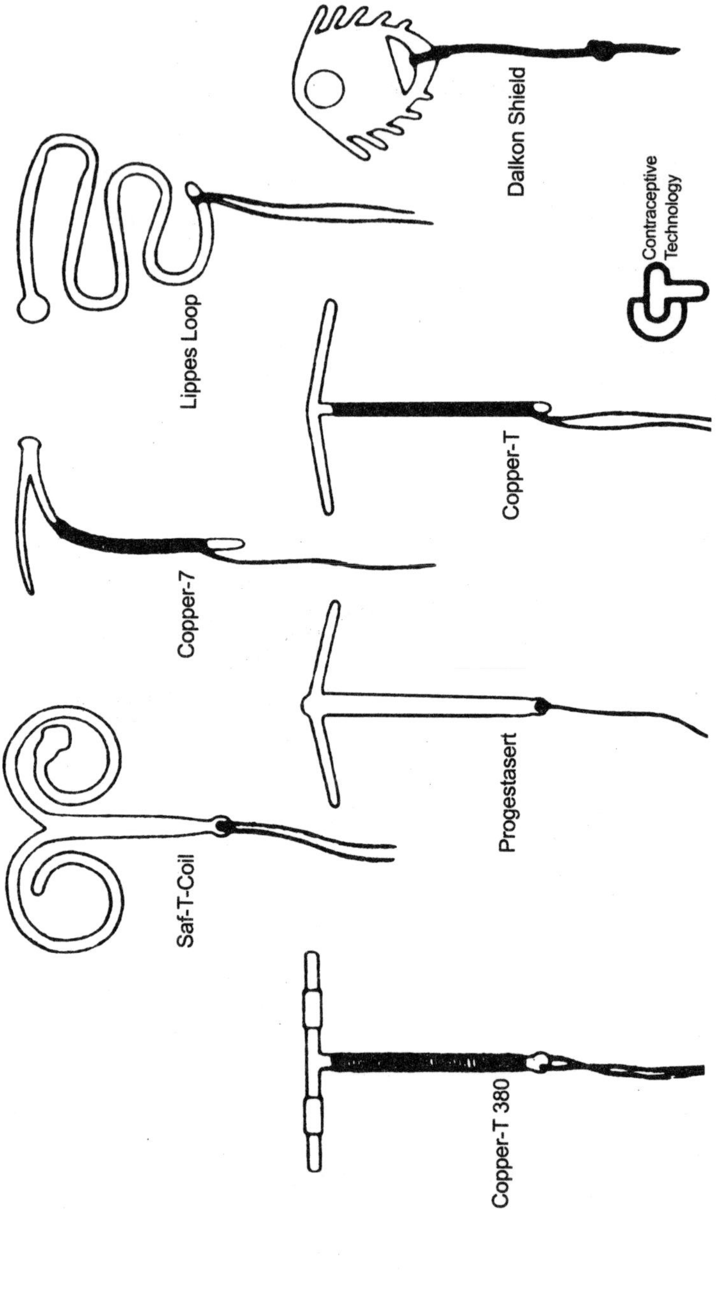

Fig. 12.1: Various available Intra Uterine Contraceptiue Devices (IUCD).

Q.7. According to cost effectiveness, classify contraceptive methods?

Ans.

	Name	Cost range in Rs. per mth.	
		Private	*Government*
1.	Abstinence	NIL	NIL
2.	Coitus interruptus	NIL	NIL
3.	Condom (Rs)	3-15	FREE
4.	Pills	30-70	FREE
5.	Injectables	175 for every 3 months	Not available
6.	Norplant	5000/- (single)	Not available
7.	IUCD [Copper-T]	300/- (single) for 3-5 yrs.	FREE
8.	Fertility awareness methods	NIL	NIL
9.	VT/TT	2000-5000 (Single)	FREE (Drugs Extra)
10.	Foam/Cream/Jelly	25-150	Not available.

Q.8. Classify the contraceptive methods according to effective usage duration?

Ans.

	Method	*Use per Intercourse*	*Lasting duration of effectivity*
1.	Abstinence	Single	Till abstinence is followed
2.	Coitus interruptus	Single	Episodic
3.	Condom	Single	Episodic
4.	Pills	Multiple	Till taken orally
5.	Injectables	Single for 3 months	Till taken regularly
6.	Norplant	Single	5 years
7.	Fertility Awareness	Single method	One month
8.	IUCD	Single	3-5 years
9.	Foam/Jelly	Single	Episodic
10.	VT/TT	Multiple	Life

Sex desire can be stimulated by seeing, listening, imagining, reading, touching or by caressing.

13

Sex Tonics

Definition

Sex Tonics (Aphrodisiacs) are chemical, herbal, natural or synthetic agents, considered to enhance sexual desire (Appetite) psychologically and improve sexual performance physically.

These agents may be foodstuffs or herbs or animal organ sources or naturally or synthetically derived drugs.

There remain a basic human urge and still an avid search for an ideal sex tonic which can increase both sexual desire and performance simultaneously.

An ideal Aphrodisiac should have:

1. No side effects.
2. Equal enhancing effect on desire and performance.
3. Specific mild to moderate effect on altering mental state for desire.
4. Specific mild to moderate effect on local genital tissue for performance.
5. Economy and easy availability.
6. Rapid and sustained onset of action.

Above-mentioned points simply assert, the ideal sex tonic still is elusive. Many Ayurvedic, herbal and medicinal products are used with the claim that they could increase a person's sexual powers or desire. A long list of such substances is being given here with questionable response on sexual desire and performance varying from person to person, race to race and from continent to continent:

1. Oysters (Sea animal).
2. Ginseng Root (Man Root).
3. Powdered Rhino's Horn.
4. Lion/Tiger/Cheetah's testicles.
5. Turtles Eggs.
6. Spanish fly.
7. Alcohol.
8. Narcotics as Heroin, Morphine.
9. Amphetamine and Cocaine.
10. Marijuana.
11. LSD.
12. Asparagus.
13. Caviar.
14. Truffles (Italy).
15. Chocolate.
16. Onions.
17. Figs.
18. Fennel.
19. Banana.
20. Licorice.
21. Anchovies.
22. Lard.
23. Scallops.
24. Raisins.
25. Dry Fruits.
26. Ashwagandha.
27. Nest-soup of a bird (Indonesia).

Vitamins have effect on general vigour of body but have no effect on sex desire or act.

The widely used and accepted Aphrodisiac among these is Alcohol. Effect of Alcohol on sexuality have astonished people all through history and will continue to do in times to come. Alcohol is known to enhance the sexual desire, by abolishing all inhibitions but doesn't improve with sexual performance. *Alcohol increases the sexual responsiveness, certainly because of lost inhibitions of the subject.*

In 1989, Food & Drugs Administration of USA declared that there is no scientific proof that any 'over the counter' Aphrodisiacs work to treat sexual dysfunction. As far other listed Aphrodisiacs are concerned, many ancient concepts and folklore believed the "law of similarity", reasoning that an object resembling genitalia may possess sexual powers. And the very similar shape of Ginseng, Rhinocerous horn, Oyster, Banana etc. are classical examples falling in the category of law of similarity.

Chemical analysis of some of Aphrodisiacs have shown very normal contents of much acclaimed libido-enhancers. Like Oyster is rich in Zinc while Rhinoceros' horn is rich in Calcium and Phosphates.

A person taking deficient diet being supplemented with loading doses of Calcium + Phosphorous from Rhino's horn and Zinc from Oyster or any other normally required mineral or trace element could improve with general physical vigor and possibly lead to an increased sexual interest.

Whatever sex arousal agents are available being acclaimed or proclaimed of modern times or since ancient times, they are having mechanism of action as under:

1. Psychological boosting up.
2. Removal of Inhibitions.
3. Improve general vigour.
4. Increase local genital blood flow by irritating the mucosa of genito-urinary tract.

Alcohol does not improve with sexual performance but enhance the sexual desire.

14

Orgasm

Definition

It is explosive feeling of sudden and intense pleasure, a physiological result of heightened sexual excitement and neuromuscular response, followed by relaxation of sexual tensions and body's muscles.

Orgasm is also called as CLIMAX or CUM.

Orgasm benefit women physically and psychologically thereby alleviating all physical, emotional, mental and psychological stresses.

Physiology of Orgasm (Fig. 14.2)

Orgasm is shortest phase of sexual response cycle, a neuromuscular state of ecstasy. To be in sexual state, sexual response start from fantasy, hearing, sight.

Smell, taste, touch or imagination use different path to stimulate the brain which is the main sex arousal centre. Activated brain centre then release impulses of sexual excitation to sex centres in spinal cord. There from male and female sexual organs become flooded with increased flow of blood, presenting erection in males and lubrication in females. Maintenance of sexual arousal into excitation and phase of plateau, leads ultimately to the state of orgasm.

Our brain is the most potent Aphrodisiac.

Orgasm is a sensation which begins with a momentary sense of suspension, quickly followed by an intensely pleasurable feeling that usually begins at the clitoris and spreads rapidly throughout the pelvis. This pelvic throbbing include muscle contraction in the vagina and in lower pelvis.

Orgasm is an energetic process comprised of a rush of intensely pleasurable feelings which is marked by:

- feeling of sudden intense pleasure, as total Body response.
- Sex flush and widespread vasoconstriction.
- Elevated uterus.
- Vagina profusely lubricated.
- Engorged breasts in females.
- Erected Nipples.
- Spasm of pelvic muscles both in males and females.
- Rhythmic vaginal contractions in females.
- Ejaculation in males.
- Involuntary vocalization.

Duration of Orgasm

Orgasm lasts for a few (2-10) seconds. It stands as single event with males and may be multiple with females while continued stimulation is given for extended period of time. The feel of orgasm vary with time, place or person. It may be explosive, ecstatic, avalanche of sensation or mild, less intense or less dramatic.

Female orgasm requires a masterly approach to attain in comparison to more frequent and easily attained male orgasm. The female orgasm presents a paradox. There can be two ways of female genital stimulation to help reach orgasm by self or by partner.

1. Clitoral stimulation.
2. Vaginal or G-spot stimulation.

Clitoral stimulation can be done with finger tip or shaft of penis or with any sex toy (clitoral stimulator) worn on the shaft of penis. Some women find the clitoral orgasm feel better if the vagina is filled simultaneously and pleasantly. This filling of vagina can be a self service with fingers or dildo/vibrators (sex-toys) or a mutual affair with male partner's penis.

Causes of Early or No orgasm

- Environmental situation.
- Fear of being seen, heard or caught.
- Intense urge leads to rapidity of act.
- Improper lubrication of reproductive organs.
- Fatigue, mental or physical.
- Fear of kids, getting awaken.
- Diseases like Diabetes.
- Psychogenic (Functional).
- Anxiety.
- Prolonged Abstinence.
- Infection, Myopathy, Neuropathy.
- Inadequate Sexual Arousal.
- Low Testosterone levels.

Learn how to delay Male Orgasm

Love making is an art. Apart from Inborn capabilities, like other skills, love-making can also be learnt effectively. With some practical approaches, Orgasm can be delayed. Let us understand how easily one can learn.

(a) **Desensitise the Glans-Penis by—**

- Wearing Double/Single condom.
- Interrupt the thursting Penis in vagina by either stopping in vagina or pulling it out and wait for a while.
- Ask your partner while you lie on the bed to get a finger/palm rubbing masturbation. At the verge of ejaculation ask your female partner to squeeze the glans

---

Masturbation is legitimate form of "sex for one".

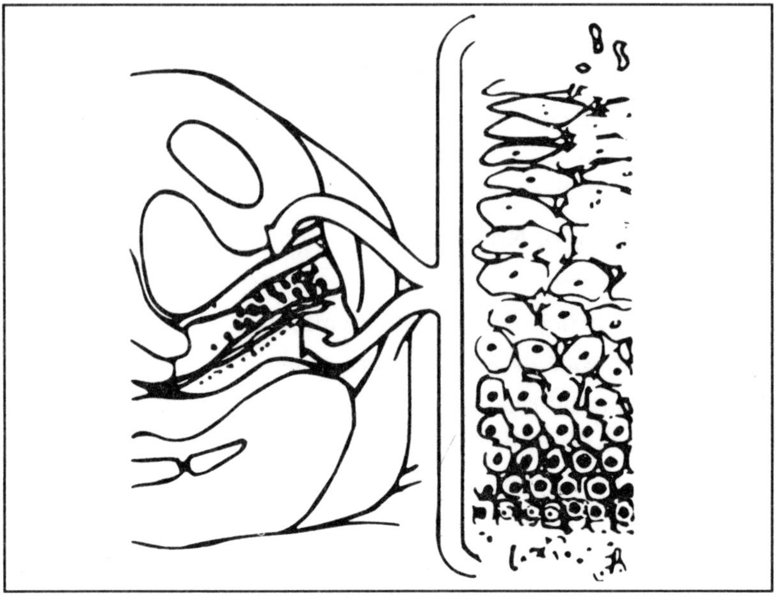

Fig. 14.1: Lubrication

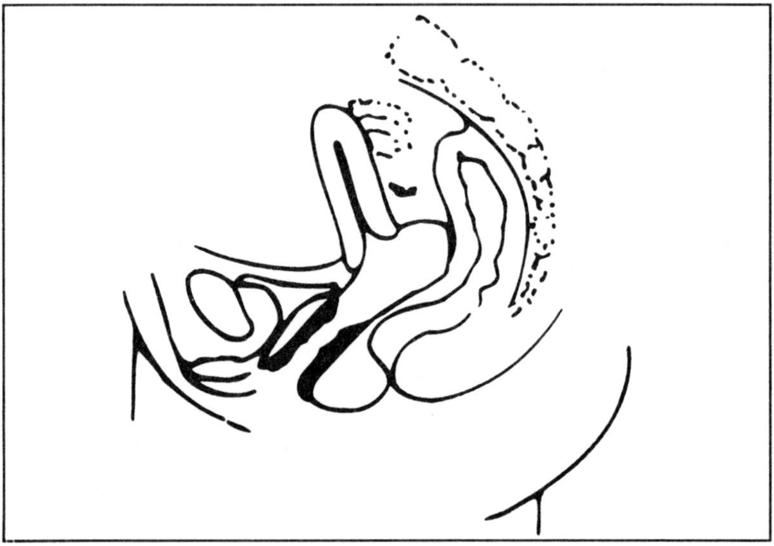

Fig. 14.2: Orgasm

Multiple G-spot orgasm is more easy to achieve than multiple clitoral orgasm.

part of Penis, so tightly, that it triggers a pain sensation through the shaft to the spine. A continuous practice may help you develop this skill of delayed ejaculation and Orgasm.

(b) **Try Different Position as—**

- Woman on top position.
- Missionary Position.
- Rear Vaginal Entry in Standing/Knee Bent Position.
- Sitting criss-cross with folded legs on each other.
- Kegel's (PC) Exercise.

To control the ejaculation through urethra, Pubococcygeus (PC) is the responsible muscle. A strong and hypertrophied P.C. Muscle will help in controlling the ejaculation while the process of Intercourse is going on. Kegel's exercise is also useful in urinary incontinence.

(c) **How to strengthen PC Muscle**

PC muscle functions to stop the flow of urine while male or female urinates. A regular pattern of contraction for about six seconds followed by relaxation will help in development of holding of ejaculation for quite some time.

(d) Do not mix Alcohol with sex as Alcohol ingestion, increases the desire of sex but takes away the performance. Alcohol clouds the judgement making about morality and safe practice of sex. The simple notion to understand is, "Either Alcohol or Sex."

Vaginal Orgasm

Vaginal orgasm is achieved due to stimulation of G-spot which is an erotic zone located on front wall of vagina along the course of urethra (urinary passage tube) that would swell during sexual stimulation.

The elusive spot is named after a German physician named Ernst Grafenburg. It has been suggested that this G-spot is nothing but counterpart of male prostate gland.

Vaginal fisting is having all or most of lover's hand in the vagina.

Male orgasm is associated with ejaculation. Ejaculation is a reflex, a glandular reflex due to pelvic muscle contraction thereby causing pumping out of fluid from prostate and seminal vesicles. Male orgasm is a sequence of physical processes which once initiated cannot be stopped without using artificial means. Male orgasm and ejaculation are not one but they occur in most cases, simultaneously. Ejaculation is discharge of semen which can be reflex due to spasm of muscles, without any feeling of orgasm.

Orgasm can be without ejaculation in

- Boys before puberty.
- Prostatic disease.
- Use of certain drugs.

Ejaculation without orgasm can be seen in neurological diseases, in males.

Campaign-A.S.K. (Attribute-Sex-Kindly)

Healthy and Morale Sex Practices	*Go slow or First Avoid Sexual Practices*	*Strict stay away Practices*
• Masturbation • Sex with spouse • Legitimate sex with condom • Oral Sex • 69 sex • Mutual Masturbation	• Illegitimate Sex with unknown sexual history • Promiscuous sex • Anal Sex • Lesbianism • Voyeurism (Peeping Tom)	• Prostitution • Group Sex • Multiple Partners • Sodomy • Homosexuality for Males • Casual Sex with unknown partner • Sex without condom • Bestiality (Sex with Animals) • Sex with Alcohole taken, as it clouds Judgement taking.

Sex is most about pleasure and intimacy rather than technique.

15

Sex Education: Present Scene, Need and Implications

In this nation of KAMA-SUTRA it has been a point of debate whether the children, young adults and teen-agers be given any education about SEX for their need and knowledge base. In the present context the only wealth possessed by this holy and old nation is just the Character and to some extent Morality. And we should look in the congruence of stability of these two important factors for set norms of Indian culture and life styles from ancient times. Though the criterion are fast changing and no established criterion last long to prove their ethnicity, relatedness and its relation to spiritualism.

The present scenario has great implications through the roots of Media from sky where truthfulness of sex and its relation to teenage group is not met with, as the crooked form of sex via the unnecessary body exposure and substandard language is downpoured over the populace. The need of proper Sex Education then comes into picture as the present young generation is exposed more to tensions and temptations of all kind in society, schools and in colleges. It is time to take lesson from Indian Tribes who run ancient traditions in provision of education for sex to their youngsters. In present context these ancient customs seem to be spiritual, timesworthy and practical to follow on. To mention, it is here that Tribes of Jhabua and Bastar (M.P.) follow a custom of GHOTUL teaching. Ghotuls are the closed community halls where teenage boys and girls of the tribe receive all sorts of lessons for life including education of sex from their respective senior and adult counterparts. These Ghotuls have been a matter of dispute as the British rulers had propagated it as practical sex training centers for entertainment possibly because of exclusiveness of these centers only to the tribal inhabitants. But one should try to get and receive positive things even out of negative attitude or so-called negative customs to follow the optimistic norm of "Cloud having a silver lining". The need is to conceptualize and develop separate sex education centers for boys and girls. These centers can be run by the panchayat level authorities at village level and by municipal corporations at the urban level. Senior citizens, aldermen and volunteers can be employed for an effective delivery for a good cause.

The set norms of non-training in the field of education in sex are also not producing any good results either. Therefore it is important and timesworthy to think in a very positive way to start providing proper sex education to our forthcoming generations. As far as Medical science is concerned there also, sex is not taught as a subject. The need is very much to train our young doctors and family physicians also to be a counsellor for prevailing myths, non-organic and organic problems which most of the times are Psychogenic in origin. This can very well be done by C.M.E. *i.e.* Continued Medical Education to all eligible doctors & para-medical staff. The criterion should be such that, Educational Institutes are provided with qualified persons to deliver lectures on sex in separate classes to males and females. This will certainly enhance and strengthen the relationship between pupils and teachers. This will help in a positive manner to the teen-ager while they pass on to their adulthood without mystery and confusion. The provision of sex education in this manner will also let down the genesis of misconception, which is being received and developed from their friends of ill knowledge and from cheap local language pornographic literature available at footpath.

Female arousal takes longer to build and can often last longer, and be more intense.

Most of the sexual disorders in India are of Psychogenic origin and in practice since last 8 years I've seen more than expected numbers of cases suffering with Dhatu rog i.e. discharge of secretions from urinal orifice in males, which possibly is prevalent only in India because of practice of squatting position. As it is a discharge of the prostate gland this is not considered as a disease with pathology. It is having no drugs to play any passive or active role in this psychogenic disability of good magnitude. Here it is well treated with a kind attention by even a family physician at grass root level through comprehensive sex education regarding brief Anatomical and Physiological exposure to the patient. Otherwise the patient becomes a money-getter to the doctor/quack by unethical medication, which are non-productive by all means.

It has been experienced that the youngsters seek and receive knowledge from their fellow friend and from cheap porn literature which do not furnish the basic and real facts of sex, thus a very mysterious, unethical and wrong picture is established on majority of teenagers. The teenagers never seek any advice from their parents or their family physicians. The parents may and should provide a basic package in this matter to prevent inflow of ingenuine information to young adults as a part of their duty. An uninformed or mis-informed youth is exposed more to arrest of emotional and psycho-sexual development resulting in genesis of sexual deviations. In number of cases the nuclear and joint family teenage candidates may get indulge in so called INCEST, possibly only because of a keen interest in knowing the very basic thing about the fellow counter sex, in the body of brother, sister, or even to mother and father. Lack of education and prevailing mis-conceptions in the youth results in Personality disorders which on being severe may produce Gender Identity Crises e.g. Trans-sexualism, which are difficult to be treated. Ignorance about sex is prevailing in all strata of society in India that is a major lacuna for healthy orgasmic sex. Sex-Education will certainly lead to a better Sexuality.

Biochemically, loss of love or grief, is inverse of love, leading to low levels of endorphins, a chemical agent known for its pain relieving effects.

The strategy to undergo for effective structure for Sex Education is as follows:

A. The basic individual school is the Home to settle the very initial queries of the kids. A male child first of all is attracted to his mother (Oedipus-complex) and a female child is inclined to her father (Electra-complex).

B. The basic individual teacher is father for boy and mother for girl. The Parents are the first educators for children and they have a moral duty to furnish basic structure and mechanism in a very conversational language and in no atypical manner.

C. There should be a satisfying answer to each valid query about sex, which should be genuinely true, in modest terminology.

D. Young individual found playing with his/her sex organ should not be discouraged. This only increases the curiosity about their own sex and to the opposite sex. Sex should not be considered as a taboo by the parents and it duly needs an open discussion.

E. Every legal question should be satisfied by means of appropriate ethical, spiritual and fundamental answer.

F. The questionnaire should never be discouraged in any way to produce confusion in mind, which may lead to development of an abnormal concept and genesis of Personality disorders in youth.

G. The Physiology of birth of baby can be explained by making simple examples of male-female plant/tree thereby explaining if possible as the Pollination take place. In my practice I've found this, the most appropriate and satisfying way to calm the childhood queries. The teenagers now are so advanced in this regard that they can, even ask/reveal their perversion also.

H. The Schools must start conducting seminars and symposiums exclusively on sex to their matriculate

---

Sexual problems in youngsters are about 80% psychological and 20% physical.

students by local qualified Physicians at least twice in a full academic session. This session can be assisted by audio-visual episode also. Adolescent growth spurt in Boys between 13-15 years and in Girls between 11-14 years. The puberty begins at the age of 12-13 years in boys and 11-12 years in girls. At this juncture of life it is must to consider a beginning in sex education.

I. A free session of questions and answers must be there between the educator and students. The girls should receive this session from a female educator only.

J. The need is to educate the sex workers who are the source of active infection for various sexually transmitted diseases & ofcourse most dreaded AIDS and Hepatitis B.

At the outset the package of sex-education should include the following for academic purposes:

1. Basic Anatomy of human body.
2. Physiology of genital functioning.
3. Common myths, misconceptions and queries in young age group are:
   (a) Masturbation,
   (b) Dhat rog (discharge of secretion),
   (c) Wet dreams,
   (d) Menstrual cycle,
   (e) Frigidity,
   (f) Ejaculation and pre-mature ejaculation,
   (g) Inclination of the organ to a side,
   (h) Pregnancy,
   (i) Orgasm,
   (j) Relation of age,
4. Common sex oriented diseases of infective and psychogenic origin and their Prevention.

For boosting sexual stamina & releasing sexual tensions practice masturbation regularly.

5. Role of Drugs/Aphrodisiac/Tonic/Anxiety and pornographic literature and alcohol in sex performance.
6. Essentials of a good sex partner.
7. Essentials of a good sex performance.
8. Preventive measures of occurrence of sexually transmitted diseases.
9. Paraphilia (sexual-deviation)

   The sexual deviations are:

   (a) Homosexuality *i.e.* receiving sexual gratification from same sex partner.

   (b) Sadism *i.e.* sexual gratification by inflicting pain to the partner.

   (c) Masochism *i.e.* sexual gratification by receiving painful stimulus from the partner.

   (d) Fetishism *i.e.* enjoying sex with the foul smell of faeces et cetra.

   (e) Exhibitionism; *i.e.* receiving sexual gratification by exhibiting whole body or part of body in public.

   (f) Voyeurism *i.e.* enjoying while seeing how an actual act is taking place by others.

   (g) Transvestitism *i.e.* gratification by dressing up with opposite sex's garments.

   (h) Pedophilia *i.e.* having sexual relation with young children.

   (i) Bestiality *i.e.* establishing sex with the animals.

The media and the electronic mass media from sky has a major role to play in provision of sex education in a very effective way by making:

1. Documentary;
2. Talk-show;
3. Scientific sessions;

Aphrodite is Greek goddess of sexual love and beauty (Aphrodisiac) counterpart of our KAM DEV.

4. Group discussions;
5. Problem oriented question/answer sessions;
6. Display banners and advertisements for disease prevention;
7. Establishment of sex education society for active participation from the Masses.

The direct effect of the sex education are well versed and understood but indirect repercussions include a limiting effect on fast growing population in India. A sex-educated person will certainly think and act positively as far as planning of family is taken into consideration. A comprehensive delivery of education in this regard may have a lower tendency of suicide in the respective age groups. Provision of sex education is a prospective measure of treatment to avoid the sexual disorders and deviations. The married couples also suffer with an untoward inclination to the use of aphrodisiacs. The so-called aphrodisiacs enhance the libido and not the performance, it is understood. *A good sex act lie in just a sound health: regular exercise and ofcourse a sound sleep pattern.*

Women characterize the clitoral orgasm as SHARPER and the G-spot orgasm as DEEPER.

16

Positions

Variety is being loved by all Human Beings. Sex or Intercourse or making love is no exception either. It is misconception that man need variety in love making and intercourse but the truth is that women also enjoy the change in position. A will to experiment and innovate with love-play keeps the enthusiasm and fun, all alive in sex and its course through the married life.

Various positions are being practiced and an unending debate will go on as what number of sex positions can be had or practiced. Even a strange thought or actual intercourse or part of it in public at a strange place may pump a dose of adrenaline into a couple living for years together. The basic patterns of Intercourse being discussed here are:

1. *Face To Face Position:*
   - Lying
   - Lying on Side
   - Both Partners Standing
   - Both Partners Sitting
2. *Rear Entry Position:*
   - Lying
   - Standing
   - Both Partners on Sides

Change of place, pattern of clothing gives on attractive stimulation and invitation for sex between husband and wife (partners).

3. *Side Lying Entry Position:*
   - Straight Sideways

Face To Face Position

Man Above and Woman Beneath

This is most commonly used position by humans through the continents. It is also known as MISSIONARY POSITION. In this position the woman lies flat on her back with her hip and knee flexed (bend) to expose the vulva. Man puts his chest on the woman's breast and inserts his organ into the vagina while his flanks are in between the thighs of the woman. This position facilitates mouth to mouth kissing but averts breast massaging and clitoral stimulation with the help of fingers.

Variation may be—

- Woman straightens her legs to spread them wide.
- Man puts his legs outside woman's and squeezes her.
- Woman lifts her legs up to keep them on Man's waist or encircle the man's flank by getting her legs across.
- Woman lifts her legs up, to keep them on Man's shoulder.
- Raise the woman's buttocks by putting a pillow below.

Woman Above and Man Beneath

While lying on the bed, woman positions herself above the Penis with her legs outside or inside Man's legs. Proper insertion of male organ in the vulva will get momentary movements of both the partners namely woman from above and man from below.

Variations May Be—

- Lifting woman's body so that man can caress her breast and watch the event which becomes more exciting.
- Woman sits with her knees & legs outside man and penis inside her. This position helps in controlling ejaculation and is practiced most in Pregnancy.
- Reverse Thrusting as woman on top receives, as man from beneath lifts her legs to wrap them round her body.

Several options are available for males to last long enough erections like penile injections, surgical implants and vaccum pump.

- Woman on top turns her body to side so that breast caressing and butt slapping (love slaps) can enlighten the exotic movements.

Both Partners Standing

Face to face standing position in love making is common as QUICKIE. Height of woman here plays a crucial role as the act is performed against the wall. For a joyful event, act can be had on the stairs. This method of intercourse is more acrobatic and need an athletic man to perform it nicely.

Variation may be—

- Man lifts the woman into the air to get her legs around the waist and the vulva just in front of the penis.
- Woman, with her legs wrapped around the man at the waist, leans back on the floor.

Lying on Side

In this, both the partners lie on their sides, facing each other and getting the penetration. Though the penetration in this position is a bit difficult but is pleasant for the persons enjoying long and slow love making fortified with conversation.

Rear Entry Position

Lying on The Bed:

This position lets the man to make an entry into vagina from behind. The basic position gets woman beneath and man above as she kneels on the bed with her head down. Man enters the vagina gently, with her both hands free enough to titillate breasts, nipples and exotic clitoris even.

Variations—

- Woman lying flat on the bed.
- Woman placed on the edge of the bed.
- Man lifts woman with holding waist at the edge of the bed, getting Head and Breast of the woman on bed and both legs hanging in air held by hubby.

DILDO are sex toys for the females very popular in West, made of silicon, are simple to clean, and give Feel Good sensation.

Standing

This interesting position gets woman bend at the waist with support of table, sofa or even chair. This standing position exposes the vulva from behind thereby giving an exciting sight and compelling a thrusting entry into the vagina. This position can give the partners an ecstatic feeling both by act and by location as in garden, bathroom, Kitchen or in Living room.

Variation

Woman remains erect in posture. Entry in this is difficult but body caressing is very easy.

Rules of Intercourse

- Desire for Sex is a natural physiological phenomenon and is ruled by Nature. MOTHER Nature has established that no male animal will stimulate or copulate the female animal unless accepted by cyclic physiological process is there. Though this rule is not true for HUMAN BEINGS as sex is basically an activity for getting the young ones. For human beings it is also an activity of Fun.
- Lust and love are different. Lust is all physical and transient while love is all mental and eternal.
- Desires leads to Lust which need avoidance by teenagers. Safe sex is the need of hour and ABSENTEEISM is the key of successful unmarried life.
- No aphrodisiac is better than:
  - Normal and Balanced Diet.
  - Sane and sound state of mind.
  - Sound sleep pattern.
  - Avoidance of over anxiety about sex.

None of addictive agent whatsoever is as prolific as is YOUTHFULNESS. Young boys and girls should understand this and don't get carried away with imposed temptation and compulsion.

G-Spot is a small coin sized highly sensitive area behind the front wall of the vagina.